Million-Dollar
WORDS

More Than 1,000 Words to
Make You Sound Like A Million Bucks

Seth Godin and Margery Mandell

Running Press Book Publishe
Philadelphia, Pennsylvania

D1015396

Canadian representatives: General Publishing Co., Ltd., 30 Lesmill Road, Don Mills, Ontario M3B 2T6.
International representatives: Worldwide Media Services, Inc., 30 Montgomery Street, Jersey City, New Jersey 07302.

ISBN 1–56138–244–2

Library of Congress Cataloging-In-Publication Number 92–50795

Cover design by Toby Schmidt
Interior design by Nancy Loggins
Cover illustration by Frank Renlie

Typography: Goudy Oldstyle by Richard Conklin
Printed in the United States

This book may be ordered by mail from the publisher.
Please add $2.50 for postage and handling.
But try your bookstore first!

Running Press Book Publishers
125 South Twenty-second Street
Philadelphia, Pennsylvania 19103

Preface

Million-Dollar Words is *Dress for Success* for your vocabulary. The words in this book—complete with guides to pronunciation for words that may be ambiguous—will make it easier for you to be precise, to say exactly what you mean. But more importantly, they will tell the world that you are a sophisticated, intelligent person with significant thoughts—and the vocabulary to make them clear.

There are more than 1,000 words in this book. The average adult American has a working vocabulary of less than 3,000 words (most of them learned by the sixth grade). Once you have mastered the words in this book, you will have increased your vocabulary by as much as 33%. Take it slow—learn three words a day and you'll be done in a year.

Just like a tuxedo or evening gown, the fancy words presented herein shouldn't be overworn. You wouldn't wear a silk smoking jacket to the Yankees game, and you shouldn't use the word *abstemious* at the diner. Be patient. Wait for your moment, then roll out the right word. Some words, like *chad*, are useful every day. Others, like *agio*, are a little harder to work into the conversation, but, when you do, are as wonderful as betting it all in Final Jeopardy and getting it right.

ACKNOWLEDGMENTS

A book like *Million-Dollar Words* requires insight and effort from a lot of people. This book wouldn't have existed without the support of Lawrence Teacher and Nancy Steele, the graceful editing, hard work, and meticulous attention to detail of Melissa Stein, and the sharp eye of Lisa B. Shelkrot.

Thanks also go to Kate Grossman and Ellen Kenny, and also to Lucy, who never hesitates to add her two cents.

Finally, thanks to Michael Cader, who liked the original concept, and to our spouses, Helene and Mark.

For
Steve and Nancy Pellowe Dennis

For
Jacob, Alix, and Katie

Million-Dollar
WORDS

A

abdabs

So nervous, you jitter and quake. One hopes that diamond cutters, professional golfers and brain surgeons don't suffer from the abdabs. Pronounce it *AB-DABS*.

abject

Extremely humiliated or debased; the bottom of the barrel. The word is most often used in conjunction with either "failure" or "poverty." The migrant farmers in Woody Guthrie songs lived in abject poverty.

ablution

A ritual cleansing. This can literally be a bath, or, more commonly, a spiritual purification. Vestal virgins probably engage in this kind of activity since they have a lot of time on their hands. Say *AB-LOO-SHUN*.

abnegate — To deny oneself something (usually something a little more serious than giving up chocolate cake). You can abnegate the religion you were born into, for example. Pronounce it *AB-NEGG-ATE*.

abrogate — To formally annul or cancel, as in a contract or a treaty, rather than a promise. Often misused to mean "breach" or "violate"—when you hear the word used that way, jump in and explain the subtle yet important distinction. "He abrogated the agreement by ripping up the contract and refusing to accept any more shipments of pineapples." Distinguish this from breaching the agreement by accepting the shipments, but refusing to pay for them.

absolution — A release from guilt, sin or sentence. More than just forgiveness, absolution implies a kind of freedom from moral responsibility. To be on the safe side, it's best to avoid acts that require absolution, since it might not be offered. Say *AB-SO-LOO-SHUN*.

abstemious — Originally defined as taking food and drink in moderation, now expanded to mean temperance in all things. Those who drink deeply from the cup of life are hardly abstemious. Pronounced AB-STEEM-EE-US.

abstruse   Complicated; difficult to comprehend. Like the theory of relativity, atonal music or the philosophers you pretended to understand in college. The next best thing to understanding Hegel would be to describe him as abstruse and move on.

acerbic   Harsh; severe; biting. Commonly used to mean sarcastic, the actual meaning is stronger. A truly acerbic wit can draw blood. Don Rickles isn't acerbic. He's too nice. It's pronounced ASS-ER-BIK.

acolyte   An attendant, assistant or novice. Not a slave, but a follower. Disciples follow a leader—acolytes empty her ashtray. A brilliant professor or an innovative employer will often attract acolytes. Pronounced AK-O-LITE.

acrimony   Biting sharpness or bitterness. It's used to describe words, attitude or disposition, not food. Old coffee is bitter; hostile divorces lead to acrimony between partners, and vice versa.

acuminate | Sharpened or tapered to a point—can be used as an adjective or verb. A candle or a sword is acuminate. The next time you need to sharpen your pencil during the SATs, raise your hand and explain that your #2 needs to be acuminated. Pronounced AH-KYOU-MIN-ATE.

adduce | To offer a series of facts that will help the recipient prove something. Therefore, you can adduce someone to deduce a conclusion. "Talented salesman that I am, I adduced the customer to my way of thinking by demonstrating how effective the Elektra was at picking up dust."

adventitious | Added accidentally, casually or from an outside source. Buying a house in winter and discovering that in spring, the property is filled with tulips and lilies is adventitious. On the other hand, being the one millionth customer at a dealership and winning a brand new Corvette is serendipitous. (See *serendipitous*.) It's pronounced AD-VEN-*TISH*-US.

aesthete | A lover of beauty. Sort of an athlete of the arts. If you belong to PBS, have a membership at the local art museum and drive a 1964 Lotus, you are both wealthy and an aesthete. Though it can be spelled esthete, the snootier spelling is aesthete. Pronounced *ESS-THEET*.

agelast A person who never laughs. Words like "dour" or "stern" are more temporary—reserve *agelast* for long-term sourpusses. Pronounced *AH-GEHL-AST*.

agent provocateur A French expression describing a political spy who provokes people to perform an illegal action that will lead to their arrest. These characters are frequently seen in 1940s spy films. Third-world governments often use them to promote riots, thus giving an excuse for martial law. Say *AGENT PROH-VAHK-OH-TYUR*.

agio The fee charged by money brokers for exchanging one foreign currency for another. Not to be confused with the Spanish word for "garlic," which is pronounced the same way. Pronounced *AH-JEE-O*.

aglet The covering at the end of a shoelace. Of all the words for a-thing-that-should-have-a-name-but-you-can-never-remember-what-it-is, this is the easiest to use in conversation.

agrypnia

Insomnia. The kind of word you stay awake trying to remember. Say AH-*GRIP*-NEE-AH.

ailurophilic

Lover of cats; the opposite of ailurophobia. Admittedly, "cat lover" is a lot easier to say, but you can use *ailurophilic* when you don't want your dog to know how you feel. Pronounced EYE-*LOOR*-A-FILL-ICK.

ait

A favorite crossword-puzzle word. A small island in a river or lake, such as Ile de la Cité in the Seine. Say ATE.

alacrity

Cheerfulness; liveliness. Good news is usually delivered with great alacrity.

aleatory

Uncertain; dependent on chance. Random, such as the throw of dice. Playing the lottery is an aleatory undertaking; playing blackjack is part aleatory, part skill. Say AYE-*LEE*-AH-TORY.

algorithm

A method for solving a mathematical problem. You can win or tie every game of tic tac toe by following a simple algorithm—start in the middle, then block any move made by your opponent. Say AL-GOH-RIH-THM.

alliaceous

Smelling or tasting of garlic or onions, such as one's breath after a great Italian meal. The alliaceous meal was delicious; her breath was not. It's pronounced AL-EE-AY-SHUSS.

alliteration

A poetic device in which words that begin with the same sound are strung together. "Helplessly hoping her harlequin hovers nearby. . . ." Score big points by identifying alliteration wherever you find it. Pronounced UH-LIT-ER-AY-SHUN.

amanuensis

A scribe; someone employed to take dictation or copy what another has written. John Milton's wife was his amanuensis; Milton dictated *Paradise Lost* to her. Many secretaries are amanuenses, but they prefer to be called administrative assistants. Say UH-MAN-YOO-EN-SISS.

ameliorate
To make a bad situation better. When something is ameliorated, it's improved. Not usually used in a medical environment; better to refer to a political or social situation. Some say that World War II helped ameliorate the effects of the Depression. Say AM-*EEL-YOR-ATE*.

amphigory
A nonsensical composition or parody, often made of sounds that imitate words and rhyme, or words that rhyme but have no logical meaning. An example is the writing of Dr. Seuss when he says about eating green eggs and ham: "Would you like them in a house? Would you like them with a mouse?" Pronounced AM-*FI-GORE-EE*.

anachronism
A person or event erroneously placed in time. Although it can be used either way, the word usually describes something from the past intruding upon the present in a contradictory or paradoxical way. Space people from the future would not usually be called an anachronism, but a person with a black-and-white TV and a gramophone would. Say AN-*AK-CROH-NISM*.

analects

Selected extracts from the writings of one or more authors. Usually associated with Confucius, as in *The Analects of Confucius*, or with Mao—although the word is by no means limited to Asian writing.

ancillary

This word is often used to mean secondary, but it actually means supplementary, as in "the ancillary benefits to this job are its good location and the friendly staff." The word is pronounced *AN-SILL-AR-EE*.

anomaly

An unexpected result that deviates from the standard. A 40-degree day in the middle of a hot summer is an anomaly, as is a book on underwater gardening that makes it to the best-seller lists. Pronounced *UH-NOM-UH-LEE*.

anomie

The breakdown of norms, ethics and values in a person or in society. Graft, corruption and rioting are all signs of anomie. Pronounced *AN-EH-MEE*.

antediluvian

This word literally means "before the Biblical flood," but it's come to connote generally ancient or antiquated. Someone with very old-fashioned ideas might jestingly be described as antediluvian. It's pronounced ANT-EE-DEL-OOV-EE-AN.

antepenultimate   The third from the last in a series; the word or thing that precedes the second to last (or penultimate) and the last. A useful word when discussing a piece of writing, as in: "It says here in the antepenultimate paragraph . . ."

anthropomorphism   Assignment of human-like attributes to inanimate objects or animals. People tend to anthropomorphise computers: "The computer gets upset when I type this." The word can be used to refer to fairy tales about singing trees and talking frogs.

antithetical   Something that is in direct opposition to something else is antithetical to it. The word has a larger meaning than just plain "opposite." Rich is the opposite of poor; booking a rap music group at a staid, elegant French restaurant would be antithetical to the restaurant's atmosphere.

aphasia   Loss or impairment of speech, or of the power to understand written or spoken language. It's rare to find a permanent case in real life, but temporary aphasia is all around us. A great excuse when your boss catches you snoozing at a meeting; she'll be too stunned to look up the word. Say UH-*FAY*-ZHUH.

aplomb

Self-assurance, especially under duress. Not a fruit, but pronounced A-*PLUM*.

apocryphal

Of doubtful authenticity; practically a fable. Not like Paul Bunyan; more like Babe Ruth calling his home run. As we have lost our ability to believe real fables, many apocryphal stories have been created about heroes such as Kennedy and Hemingway.

apogee

Refers to the point in the orbit of the moon when the moon is furthest from the earth, but has come to refer to any figurative high point or climax, as in a career. Being elected President would be the apogee of a politician's career; failing to be re-elected would be the nadir. (See *nadir*.) Say *APP*-OH-JEE.

aposiopesis

Breaking off in the middle of a statement upon suddenly realizing that someone's feelings are hurt or about to be hurt. "The reason I didn't invite your wife to the party is that everybody thinks she's...well, never mind." You may never find occasion to actually use the word, but it's nice to know there's a word for that particular gaffe or faux pas. (See *gaffe* and *faux pas*.) Pronounce it *AP-UH-SEE-UH-PEE-SISS*.

apostasy

Abandonment of one's religion, politics or principles. Not to be confused with *apostle*. St. Matthew was an apostle; Judas was an apostate.

apothegm

A pithy saying. Mark Twain specialized in them. So did Yogi Berra. Say it *APP-O-THEM*.

a priori

Proceeding from cause to effect; reasoning from a general law to a particular instance. This describes a deductive approach to a chain of reasoning. If the polar ice caps melted, your a priori conclusion would be the eventual flooding of coastal areas. A second meaning is "presumptive" or "conjectural"—based on theory or preconception rather than fact, as in an *a priori* conclusion. Pronounced *AH PREE-OR-EE*.

argot

Slang belonging to a specific group or class. When you know the argot of computers, you can talk with the hackers in the MIS department. Pronounced *AR-GOH*.

arriviste
Someone who has acquired success by dubious means and who insists on flaunting it. A contemporary example would be Ivan Boesky, John Gotti or even Jessica Hahn. Unless they go to jail, one generation's arrivistes are another's old money.

arrogate
To claim for oneself without justification, such as Germany arrogating the Sudetenland prior to World War II. Can you arrogate the plum assignments from your rival co-worker?

ascetic
Self-denying; austere. A hedonist loves pleasure; an ascetic shuns it. In Eastern culture, ascetics eschew (see *eschew*) anything not necessary to maintain life, thus taking them one step closer to nirvana. (See *nirvana*.) Pronounced *UH-SETT-IK*.

assiduous
Persevering and careful. A good quality for scientific researchers or investigative reporters. The implication is that assiduous behavior brings with it thoroughness and even temper. Not necessarily true.

assonance

Describes two words in which the vowels rhyme but the consonants don't—such as *mama* and *dada*. Without *assonance*, you've got no other way to describe it!

assuage

To relieve or ease. Through good works, charity and good behavior, you can assuage your guilt about fudging your income tax report. But that probably won't save you from an audit. (See also *absolution*.) Pronounced ASS-*WAGE*.

atavistic

Exhibiting traits of an ancestor or an earlier evolutionary form. Members of a mob can become atavistic and commit violent acts which, as individuals, they might shun. A smart way to say "barbaric."

augment

To add on, in the sense of increasing in size or amount. A person augments his salary with a moonlighting job, or augments a collection of stamps by buying the valuable one with the upside-down airplane on it. You can also augment parts of your body, hence the term "breast augmentation surgery."

augur
: To prophesy the future. When Boris Yeltsin took over the USSR, it did not augur well for the KGB. (Is this word ever used without "well" attached to it?) Pronounced AWG-ER.

autodidact
: A person who teaches himself a subject, such as a foreign language or solid geometry. The word can also refer to a person who enjoys hearing himself talk even though few others do. Maybe it's because he's so smug for having taught himself something without the help of experts.

autolatry
: Worship of the self. The next time you want to insult that narcissistic, self-involved egomaniac you know, tell him he engages in autolatry. Pronounce it AWT-OL-AH-TREE.

avatar
: The incarnation or manifestation of a deity or an idea. An example is the burning bush or the Greek gods appearing in human form. Today, you could use the word to describe a project that embodied your ideas. The space program was JFK's avatar. No doubt *avatar* will end up being a make of car before long.

avocado

Of course you know what an avocado is. But did you know that it is one of the few words derived from the Aztec? The original meaning is "testicle," so now you have something interesting to say when you're offered guacamole. (The Aztecs thought the avocado was an aphrodisiac.) Also worth noting: You can keep your guacamole from turning brown by placing an avocado pit in it.

avuncular

Like an uncle; kind. Here's the hard part—what do you call someone who's like an aunt? Av*aunt*ular? Regardless, try to be avuncular to all of the children you meet.

B

babbitt

A reference to the eponymous (see *eponymous*) title of Sinclair Lewis's best-known novel, the word has come to mean a person who blindly conforms to middle-class standards. Until recently, a male babbitt always drove a four-door American car, belonged to the Lions club, wore a dark suit and went to church every Sunday.

babelize

To make something confused or incomprehensible— derived from the biblical Tower of Babel. If you earn an advanced degree in your ability to babelize, you can be certain of a job at the IRS.

bacchanal

A drunken, riotous orgy, or anyone who parties in the style of the Roman god Bacchus. You can refer to party revelers as bacchanals or to the party itself as a bacchanal. No place for abstemious (see *abstemious*) people. Pronounced *BAHK-AH-NAL*.

badinage

Playful, teasing banter, the kind of conversation that makes English drawing-room comedy so much fun to watch, even though there's no action. Best done by Tracy and Hepburn. Pronounced *BAH-DEH-NAHJ*.

Baedeker

A publisher of very good travel books. The word has come to describe any complete travel guide. Pronounced *BAY-DIK-ER*.

bagatelle

An unimportant trifle. (Not a loaf of French bread.) It's best used to describe a knickknack or a small good deed.

bailiwick

In one's area of interest or authority; the word derives from the area in which a bailiff, a minor court officer, presides. When the V.P. of Sales starts walking around the factory, complain that she's stepping into your bailiwick. Say it *BALE-EE-WIK*.

baleful

Extremely harmful; pernicious. Often confused with *doleful*, which means sad. The children in Keane paintings have doleful expressions; Roy Cohn's approach to his fellow human beings was baleful. It's pronounced *BAIL-FULL*.

balletomane A ballet-lover, who for some reason is not called a balletophile. While we're on the topic, if a female ballet star is called a ballerina, why don't they call Barishnykov a ballerino? (Just wondering.) Pronounced BAH-*LET*-EH-MANE.

baluster One of the series of pillars that supports a banister along a staircase. (Now you don't have to call it a *thingee* any longer!)

balustrade A banister plus all the balusters (see above) that hold up the banister. Pronounced BAL-UH-STRAYDE.

barm Another word for the froth or head on a glass of beer. As in: "On a hot day, there's nothing like an ice cold beer with a good barm."

bas-relief A sculpture or carved work in which projecting parts stand out slightly from their surrounding surface. When touring European cities for the first time, you may use this word about 400 times a day to describe carved doors, walls, pedestals, graves and a host of other ruins. If you're going to use the word, make sure you pronounce it correctly: BAH REE-LEAF.

bathos
A fall from the sublime to the commonplace; often used to describe the plot of a play, a movie or a piece of fiction which tells how the mighty have fallen. Pronounced BAY-THOSS, the word should be distinguished from pathos (see *pathos*), which means evoking genuine pity or compassion.

battologize
To write or repeat words or phrases over and over and over and over, again and again and again and again. It's pronounced BAT-*OLL*-OH-JIZE.

bauhaus
Not a place to put Fido at night. A school of architecture and design developed in Germany in 1918, which emphasized the functional aspect of objects over their form. The style is typified by the box-like buildings of Mies Van der Rohe, who was famous for his aesthetic theory that "less is more." Say *BOW*-HOUSE.

bavardage
Foolish or nonsensical talk with a touch of light banter. Friends might engage in bavardage by hurling meaningless insults at one another—without hurting anyone's feelings. It's similar to badinage (see *badinage*) but has a more playful tone. In modern

parlance, "dissing," but without malice. Pronounce the word BAH-VAR-*DAJ*.

beau geste   Literally a "pretty gesture," an act that is meaningless, but looks good or has the effect of generosity or conciliation. An example is sending flowers to the host after a dinner party. Pronounced BO *JHEST*.

beaver   Besides the busy little animal that builds dams, this word also describes the piece of a suit of armor that is jointed below the ears and protects the mouth and chin.

bedizen   To vulgarly dress or gaudily accessorize; too many bangles and beads. Pronounced BIH-*DYE*-ZEN.

beldam   An ugly, old woman. Not to be confused with *bedlam*, which means "confusion."

bel-esprit   A verbal, witty, intellectually lively person; the person at the party who's telling an amusing little story to a circle of delighted hangers-on. The personality shy people covet. Pronounce the word BELL-ESS-*PREE*.

bellwether
The leader of the pack; the one everyone else follows. Contrary to popular belief, the word has nothing to do with the weather—which is why it is so frequently misspelled. It does, however, have something to do with bells, since the word comes from the male sheep which leads the flock and usually wears a bell around his neck.

benighted
Ignorant; not so much stupid, but backward. People who are benighted are also a bit pathetic, such as the street urchins in Dickens's novels who, neglected by society, can neither read nor write.

benthos
The animals and plants, snails, anemones and such that live at the bottom of the sea. Not much of a stretch to use the term to vilify the telephone operator who just cut you off.

betimes
Early, soon; often misused to mean "sometimes." "I will be there betimes" means "I'll see you soon."

bibelot
A small decorative object that is prized for its beauty or rarity; the kind of porcelain figurine or little brass

pot that decorates a coffeetable or bookcase. Better than a knickknack. Pronounced *BIB-LO*.

biblioclast

A person who destroys books; the word can also be used to describe people who break the bindings of paperbacks and keep their place by folding down the corners of pages. Biblioclasts are despised by *bibliophages*, people with a passion for reading.

bibulous

Given to drinking alcohol, but not necessarily an alcoholic; for example, the person at the table who orders wine or beer when everyone else has ordered a soda. It's pronounced *BIB-YOU-LUSS*.

bifurcate

To split into two parts or branches; to fork. Though you can say that a road is bifurcated, and you can certainly bifurcate a crab before you eat it, the word is most often used to describe ideas or concepts. Pronounced *BYE-FUR-KATE*.

biggin

The perforated basket that contains the grounds in a coffeepot. The word can probably be stretched to mean the plastic holder where you put the paper filter in a Mr. Coffee.

bildungsroman | Literally, a novel of education—a coming-of-age story. J.D. Salinger's novel *Catcher in the Rye* is a classic example.

billet-doux | A love letter. Take a minute to send one today—you'll be amazed at the difference it makes in your relationship. It's pronounced BILL-AY DOO.

biotic | Having to do with life, in a scientific sense. You can be worried about the ecology, the rainforests, the ozone layer or the biotic activity in the Pacific Northwest. People on macrobiotic diets apparently believe that they are getting enormous amounts of life, which is odd, given that they eat almost nothing and weigh even less.

birl | A nifty way to say "logrolling." Standing on a log while it revolves under you. Or, stretching a little, what a gerbil does in one of those exercise wheels: "Henry! Come watch the little gerbil birl!"

bisextile | A good deal more mundane than *bisexual*, this word refers to events that fall on February 29, the extra day of a leap year. If you have a bisextile birthday, you'll age only 25 years each century. Pronounced BYE-SEX-TILL. You may not use this word often, but when you do, you'll feel great.

bivouac
An encampment, used either as a noun or a verb. Soldiers bivouac a lot, as do characters in Hemingway novels. Say *BIV-OO-ACK*.

blandish
To try to convince with flattering words; to cajole. One may blandish a child to get out of a swimming pool on a hot day. The word has nothing to do with being bland or boring.

blowzy
Unkempt; messy. Hair out of place or an untucked shirt hanging out of a business suit qualify as blowzy. Can also mean "ruddy-faced and flushed." Rhymes with *lousy*.

bluestocking
A woman who devotes herself to scholarly or literary pursuits but who is not necessarily formally educated. Think of the schoolteacher in all of those Clint Eastwood westerns. The expression comes from a group of 18th-century women who gathered in each other's houses to talk about books. Some of these

women wore informal blue or gray wool stockings instead of black silk ones.

boondoggle   Though the word is now used to describe the kind of conventions that are held in tropical places to give employees a chance for some paid vacation time, the word literally means "busy work," meaningless tasks carried out laboriously to create the appearance of being busy.

bootless   Useless; fruitless; to no avail. Thus the line from Shakespeare's sonnet ". . . and trouble deaf Heaven with my bootless cries" does *not* refer to someone praying with his shoes off.

boulevardier   A man-about-town; the kind of guy who makes sure he's seen at the trendiest restaurants and the hippest clubs. The model/artist/fashion set. Pronounced BOOL-A-VAR-*DEER*.

bovine   Scientists use this phrase to classify the family that includes buffalo, kudus, oxen and cows. Often used derogatorily to describe fat, lazy dullards who move slowly and always seem to be chewing their cuds. Pronounced *BO-VINE*.

bowdlerize

To edit a piece of writing by cutting out all the obscene parts. In certain Middle Eastern countries, some Western magazines are bowdlerized from cover to cover. The word derives from the name of Thomas Bowdler, who had the gall to issue an expurgated edition of the works of that well-known pornographer, William Shakespeare. Pronounced *BOD-LEHR-ISE*.

bromide

A trite or hackneyed remark or a boring person who speaks in meaningless platitudes. Political candidates, bad teachers and dull members of the clergy are famous for uttering (or being) bromides. Also used to describe a drink taken to relieve indigestion. Thus, depending on the intended meaning, a bromide can either soothe or turn one's stomach.

bruin

A bear. People who call their office "work-o-rama" and their friend Bill "the Billster!" probably refer to Yogi Bear as a "bruin." You can tell them that the term comes from the Dutch word for "brown," and that Bern, Switzerland, is named after the Swiss word for bear.

brussels sprout Some people like this tiny cabbage-like vegetable. Note that it is not *brussel* sprout, which is what less careful people might call it. A huge bowl of the stuff would thus be called *brussels sprouts*. Difficult to say quickly, but correct nonetheless.

bumptious Overbearing or self-assertive to the point of being obnoxious; conceited bordering on arrogant. Salespeople in trendy, expensive shops can be bumptious. Pronounced *BUMP-SHUSS*.

C

cabal
A group engaged in secret plotting against authority. A cabal might be a political faction that scorns the government, or a splinter group of employees dissatisfied with the head of their department. Often associated with witches. Pronounced *KUH-BAHL*.

cache
A hidden treasure. Not the kind found in chests under the sea but of more personal value, such as a cache of chocolates in a night-table drawer or a cache of sharpened pencils hidden from coworkers. For some reason, police always seem to find guns hidden in caches. Pronounced *CASH*.

cachet
A mark of distinction, a stamp of approval by a recognized authority. Could be the Levi's label or Louis Vuitton luggage. The word has come to describe a certain style which someone always seems to have. Pronounced *CASH-AY* or *CASH-AY*.

cachinate

To laugh too loud or too hard. Much more than a giggle, and with a bit of unnatural excess, such as nervous laughter after hearing bad news. Good example of onomatopoeia (see *onomatopoeia*). Pronounced CAK-*IN-ATE*.

cadence

A balanced, rhythmic flow or movement. You can talk about the cadence of a marching band, for example, or use the term figuratively, to describe art or a babbling brook. Pronounced KAY-*DENSE*.

cadre

A group of people who train others in an expanding organization. Often used in a military context: "Cadres of medical personnel were sent to the field hospitals." During the 1950s, Communists always seemed to be organized in cadres. Pronounced CAH-*DRA*.

caitiff

A despicable lowlife; a contemptible or cowardly person. Should be pronounced CAY-*TIFF*, probably through clenched teeth, with a sneer. Reserve the term for traitors and people who hurt others to further themselves.

cajole   To coax or encourage, usually to get someone to do
          something she doesn't want to do but that's good for
          her, such as take her medicine or get some rest. Say
          CAH-*JOLE*.

callow   Green; inexperienced; lacking maturity. You almost
          always hear the word combined with "youth," as in
          "Those callow youths don't appreciate the finer
          things in life."

calumny   A false statement designed to harm someone's
          reputation. It's intentional and malicious but has no
          particular legal implications like libel or slander. A
          jealous person might accuse a rival, or a candidate
          might accuse an opponent, of calumny.

camber   To arch upward in the middle. A rainbow cambers;
          so does a gentle hill. Downhill skis are cambered—
          the center is a few inches higher than the tip or heel.
          Pronounced CAM-*BURR*.

cambist   A classy way to describe someone who is a little too
          sharp with money. A currency trader or a particularly

zealous auctioneer is a cambist. Every school has at least one kid who manages to trade each item in his bagged lunch for some combination of cash and pizza. He's a cambist.

campanile

A bell tower that is usually separate from surrounding buildings. Far more common in Europe than in the States. The preferred pronunciation is KAM-PUH-NEE-LEE.

canard

A rumor, sham, false report or playful hoax—though less ominous than the *War of the Worlds* radio broadcast. You could accuse someone of perpetrating a canard about the state of your business.

canonize

To include in a definitive collection—especially refers to written works. The works of Chaucer have been canonized; multiculturalists have been arguing to canonize the works of minority writers. One can speak of being included among the canon of great poets, for instance. Also used to describe the process of transforming ordinary people into saints. Pronounced CAN-NON-IZE.

canorous
: Pleasant-sounding, melodious and resonant. Could be used to describe organ music, or the sound of a rainstorm against the windowpanes. It may sound like cantankerous (cranky), but means something completely different. Pronounced CAN-OR-US.

caparison
: To dress sumptuously; to gussy up. Although the word originally referred to the ornamental covering for a horse, it has come to be used for people as well, such as when heads of state get fully caparisoned for a ball at the White House. Say KUH-PAR-UH-SUHN.

capriccio
: Not an Italian coffee. A capriccio is a frolic or caper, such as when a bunch of friends spontaneously decide to jump into a car and drive to the beach for the day. Pronounced CAP-REE-SHE-O.

captious
: Critical and hard to please in an irritable, nit-picking way. Small children can be captious at the dinner table; teenagers and in-laws may be captious all the time. Say CAP-SHUSS.

carapace
: The tough upper part of the turtle's shell. The carapace is the part that used to be polished and used

for jewelry, combs and precious objects before turtles were threatened with extinction and the practice was outlawed in most countries. The word is sometimes used metaphorically to mean the demeanor of extremely self-protective people—or the pate of a bald man. Pronounced *CAH-RAH-PISS.*

carrel
A small area in a library reserved for individual study. Most carrels contain a desk, chair and lamp. (After devising such a ridiculous place for studying, scholars even went so far as to *name* it!)

caryatid
An architectural support column in the form of a draped female figure—the kind of structure, often seen in museums and Greek ruins, that resembles the Venus de Milo. (Not a bug; that's a katydid.) Pronounced *CAR-EE-AH-TID.*

castrophenia
Believing that your thoughts are being stolen by your competitors. Screenwriters often suffer from castrophenia when they see that the movie they were just about to write has appeared in neighborhood theaters. Not *Castrophilia*—that's love of Fidel Castro, in case you were interested.

catafalque The raised platform that holds a coffin containing a corpse during funeral ceremonies. A funeral is no place to show off your vocabulary, though, so you'll have to be content to know that you *could* show off, if you were so inclined. Pronounced CAT-*A-FALK*.

catharsis Originally referred to the emotional release, the necessity of which was created by Greek tragedy. Catharsis has come to mean any purging or release of emotions. Crying at the movies is considered cathartic. A debate continues to rage over whether violent movies offer catharsis—do they decrease violence among viewers or encourage it? Pronounced CAH-*THAR-SIS*.

catholic A broader meaning than "relating to the Christian church," catholic also means broad-minded or universal in tastes or views. Someone with catholic tastes might like both Beethoven and Madonna, Chinese food and coq au vin, Shakespeare and Stephen King.

cavil To nit-pick or make small-minded criticisms or objections. An old-fashioned teacher might cavil at the way his students dress; a scholar might cavil at the latest novel of a professor-turned-best-selling-author. Pronounced *KAV-EL*.

celerity

Speed or rapidity; a boy who eats his celery with great celerity gobbles his food; a student who does her homework with celerity probably makes a lot of mistakes. Celebrities who marry with celerity often find themselves with expensive divorce suits on their hands.

cerulean

Deep blue, such as the color of the sky on a sunny day, the water off the coast of a Greek island, or Paul Newman's eyes. Not mentioned in the Crayola 64 crayon box. Pronounced *SEH-RULE-EE-IN*.

chad

The little paper circles that fall from the hole-puncher and litter the floor, stick to your shoes and create static electricity that makes them almost impossible to scoop up. Used daily, this word is bound to improve your image.

chaff

Generally used to mean the leftovers, the worthless part that remains after you've got what you want.

Back when we were agrarian, the word referred to the stuff left over after harvesting wheat.

changeling

An infant, usually strange or ugly, substituted for another in the crib or in the nursery. Most often read about in fairy tales, but can be used when someone you know acts unusually, as in: "I've never seen you eat peanut butter before. Are you a changeling?"

charlatan

A fake or a phony; a person who claims to have skills, powers or talents that he doesn't possess, like a man without a medical degree who claims he's a doctor and says he can cure baldness. Pronounced *SHARL-AH-TIN*.

charnel

A house or building in which skeletons or bodies are deposited. Fortunately, it's difficult to find one these days. Pronounced *CHAR-NL*.

charrette

An effort to meet a deadline for some task by an all-out effort. Originally connoting the energy among a group of architects getting plans ready for a presentation, the word has come to refer to any group of professionals who get together and hustle to meet a due date. Pronounced *SHAH-RET*.

chary
: Cautious; hesitant to act. Use *chary* when you mean "discreetly careful" more than "wary." One would be chary before investing in a risky stock or walking into a room full of screaming sixth-graders. Pronounced CHAIR-*EE*.

chasm
: A huge gap or deep hole. "Bored with life, he leaped into the chasm." It can also be used figuratively to describe a gulf—the chasm between rich and poor, for example. Say KAZ-*M*.

chasmophile
: A lover of nooks and crannies. Someone who likes sifting through the shelves of used-book stores, rummaging through flea markets and browsing in antique stores is probably a chasmophile. So are chipmunks, mice and an assortment of other field animals who nest in the rafters of old attics. It's pronounced KAZ-*MOH-FILE*.

cheap-jack
: A peddler who sells cheap goods, like the people who sell underwear or tin earrings or inexpensive sunglasses at a flea market.

cheechako   A greenhorn; not an insult, merely a different way of
               calling someone "inexperienced" or "new to the
               scene." The word has an excellent mouth feel, and
               will add sparkle and spice to your vocabulary. Say
               CHIH-CHAH-KOH.

chimera   A mythological monster with the head of a lion, the
               body of a goat and the tail of a serpent. The word has
               come to connote any horrible fear or morbid terror.
               The day before an exam, a student is liable to imag-
               ine any number of chimeras such as not knowing the
               answer to a single question, or receiving the lowest
               failing grade on record. Pronounce it *KIM-EER-AH*.

choplogic   Faulty reasoning, often overly complicated and
               confusing. (Not Freddy Kruger's mental state.)

chrysalis   The pupa of a butterfly. The word has come to
               connote any person or thing in the process of being
               born. An adolescent on the verge of self-discovery
               could be in a chrysalis state; a novel in the early
               stages of creation could be called a chrysalis. Pro-
               nounced *CHRISS-A-LISS*.

cicatrix — Not what happens when a kid gets tired of his favorite breakfast cereal; it's the scar that forms on a healed wound, the marks from childhood mishaps that cover the knees of most adults. It's pronounced *SIK-A-TRIKS*.

cicerone — A guide who escorts tourists or sightseers, such as the gondoliers of Venice or the people who lead walking tours in most cities. Pronounced *SISS-A-RO-NEE*.

circumlocution — A roundabout way of saying something; using too many words and complicated expressions. A person who wants to avoid answering certain questions or offering certain opinions is inclined to use circumlocution. A good way of disguising choplogic (see *choplogic*). Pronounced *SIR-KUM-LOH-CU-SHUN*.

circumscribe — To create limits or define boundaries; to establish definite means or procedures. At recess, for example, children can play in circumscribed ways: they can throw balls but not rocks; they can play tag but not hit each other. Also, the scope of your research might be circumscribed by the availability of time or money. Pronounced *SIR-kum-scribe*.

clamjamfry	Ordinary people or the collective mob; politicians walk among the clamjamfry to shake hands and kiss babies. Pronounce the word CLAM-*JAM*-FREE.
clarion	A shrill-sounding trumpet used as a signal in war. The word has come to be used metaphorically to describe any obvious warning of things to come— often a bad event. "When the guest arrived and rearranged the furniture in the guest room, it was a clarion call that a difficult visit was ahead." Pronounced CLARE-*EE*-ON. (See also *warison*.)
clemency	Mercy or forgiveness, especially in choosing punishment. "The judge displayed clemency in letting the thief go free because it was his first offense." "The students begged the teacher for clemency when they were caught cheating on the final exam." Because clemency conveys mildness, the word is also used to describe the weather: clement weather is perfect for a bike ride; *inclement* weather is generally stormy.
clerisy	Intelligentsia; the collective group of educated people. In order to be a member of the clerisy, it helps to know what the word means.

clinomania The overwhelming desire to stay in bed. For some reason, mild cases seem to occur most often on rainy Sunday mornings. Say *CLINN-OH-MAY-NEE-AH*.

clinquant Glittering, from gold or tinsel. Christmas trees are clinquant, as is Zsa Zsa Gabor. What an appropriate sound the word has: *CLINK-EHNT*.

clock Decorations along the sides of socks or stockings. The little argyles that sock manufacturers are fond of weaving into men's socks are clocks. The next time someone scares you, you can say, "You scared the clocks off my socks!"

cloy To overdo and become nauseating; may be used as a verb and an adjective. Candy that is too sugary may cloy; people who are unnecessarily sweet or overly sensitive are cloying.

cockalorum A conceited, self-important, pretentious person. Be careful in your use of this word, or you'll become one.

coeval Contemporary; of the same time period. Bell-bottoms and love beads are coeval, so are two 30-year-olds. Pronounced *COH-EE-VAL*.

colloquy   Conversation, more like a formal dialogue than a casual chat. The kind of thing that goes on between a talk show host and his guest, or between two speakers at a symposium; hence the academic word *colloquium*. One doesn't usually have a colloquy with a friend on the telephone. Pronounced *CAHL-OH-KWEE*.

colophon   Not a brand of cookware. The page at the end of a book that describes the typeface used. In this age of desktop publishing, they're coming back in style. Also a publishers' emblem or trademark. Say *KAHL-AH-FAHN*.

compendious   It may sound as if the word means "big" and "encyclopedic" but it really means the opposite: concise, expressed in compact form—like *Monarch Notes* of the classics.

complaisant   Obliging and eager to please. Even though they're pronounced the same, don't confuse with complacent, which means self-satisfied and smug. A complacent person would probably expect to be served by a complaisant person.

concupiscence   A fancy way of saying sexual desire or lust, with undertones of fertility. Like pulchritude (see *pulchritude*), the word won't help you get a date. But if you're going to use it, pronounce it correctly: CON-CYOOP-*IH-SENSE*.

consanguinity   A formal way of expressing blood ties or kinship. It does not denote specific relationships (such as "sister" or "cousin"), but rather a family connection. A family tree traces consanguinity. It's pronounced CON-SANG-*GWIN-IT-EE*.

contretemps   A regrettable situation that leads to embarrassment, such as begging off a date by claiming sickness and then bumping into the canceled date at a restaurant on the same night, or making two appointments for the same time and having both show up at once. Pronounced KON-*TRA-TON*.

contumacious   Stubbornly rebellious against authority—not just irreverent, but downright disobedient. A child who refuses to stop talking during class after being asked twice is contumacious. Say KAHN-*TOOM-AY-SHUSS*.

coruscate | Sparkling or gleaming. A lake's surface coruscates in the sunlight, so does a newly washed car. The word can also be used figuratively. Someone with a lot of sparkle possesses a coruscating wit.

cosset | To spoil by coddling or excessively pampering. You can cosset a child by carrying him instead of letting him walk.

cozen | To defraud or trick. Usually less serious than down-right fraud. Scalpers cozen their clients by charging outrageous rates for last-minute tickets. Rhymes with *dozen*: CUZ-*IN*.

craven | Very cowardly, with a connotation of moral disapproval. A craven liar doesn't have the courage to admit the truth about something. Pronounced CRAY-*VEN*.

crepuscular | Lit by twilight; dusky. Though it has an ugly sound, the word usually evokes a faintly romantic darkness, such as "the mountains crepuscular in the setting sun." The lighting in certain dim restaurants is crepuscular. Pronounced CREH-*PUSSK-U-LAR*.

curmudgeon

A mean-spirited, ungenerous, irritable nasty-face who usually has no sense of humor. Hitler was evil. Scrooge was a curmudgeon.

cygnet

A young swan. Often used to describe a particularly beautiful young woman. It's pronounced *SIG-NIT*.

cynosure

The center of attention—usually a person who becomes the main attraction and directs everyone else's focus. Elizabeth Taylor at a cocktail party, for example. Pronounced *SYE-NEH-SHUR*.

D

dactyl
A finger or a toe. You have twenty dactyls; most birds have six. Pterodactyls had three-toed feet (get it?). Rhymes with *fractal*.

dada
A movement of art that hypothesized, "since art is everything, everything is art." That's why there are urinals and baseballs on exhibit in art museums. Not limited to the visual arts; use *dada* to describe any approach that is silly, stupid or ridiculous. Assonant with *mama* (see *assonnance*).

daymare
Yes, this is a word, and it means an anxiety attack—kind of like a nightmare during the daytime.

dearth
A shortage or scarcity. Squirrels might have a dearth of nuts by the end of the winter. Single women might complain of the dearth of heterosexual single

men who are sensitive and willing to make a commitment.

deciduous

Dropping off after a period of growth, such as leaves, teeth or hair. The opposite of a deciduous tree is an evergreen. Except for the rare deciduous evergreen tree, which confuses everything. It's pronounced *DEH-SID-YOU-US*.

declassé

Low-class in appearance, manners or taste; the word is generally reserved for those sufficiently upper-class to consider calling others low-class. Also used by the upper class to describe fashion that has become dated. Pronounced *DAY-CLASS-AY*.

decorous

Proper, elegant in behavior and attitude. The proper decorum at a wedding does not include making bird calls or doing your Rodney Dangerfield imitation (regardless of how good it is). Pronounced *DECK-OR-US*.

decry

To put down someone or something; to speak or write about a situation in a way that reveals regret, outrage or anger. One decries pollution of the environment or a political injustice.

de facto   Actually existing; a matter of fact. If the president of the company is on his yacht, the vice president becomes the de facto leader of the company. On the other hand, if the president of the company is on the vice-president's yacht, he becomes the de facto captain. Say *DEH FACT-OH*.

defenestration   To throw out the window—what you sometimes feel like doing with whining children. It seems that such an important-sounding word should mean something else, which is why people will be stunned when you use it properly. Pronounced *DEE-FENN-EH-STRAY-SHUN*.

dégagé   Not emotionally involved; more of an emotional state than merely being intellectually objective. A friend listening to an argument between other friends is dégagé. An umpire or a referee or a judge is at least meant to be dégagé. It's pronounced *DAY-GAH-JAY*.

demagogue   Usually refers to a politician or a leader who gains power by playing on the emotions of his constituents; there's an element of charisma and danger in it. Adolf Hitler was a demagogue. Pronounced *DEM-AH-GOG*.

demijohn

A narrow-necked bottle with wicker basket-work woven around it, like the empty bottles of Chianti that become candleholders on red-checked tablecloths in Italian restaurants.

demimondaine

A fallen woman; a woman who has lost her good reputation by a foolish or indiscreet action. Pronounced DEMI-MON-*DANE*.

depredate

To plunder. Rome suffered depredation at the hands of Attila the Hun.

de profundis

A Latin phrase for "out of the depths." Someone is pulled *de profundis* from sleep, meditation or thought. It has nothing to do with "profound," which makes the word an excellent excuse for why you weren't paying attention to whomever was speaking to you. Pronounced *DAY* PRO-*FUND-ISS*.

deracinate

To uproot in a big sense. Plants are uprooted; families or whole cultures are deracinated. The African slave trade deracinated thousands of persons. Pronounced DEE-*RASS-IN-ATE*.

descry
: To see or discover something, after careful observation. A flock of birds on the horizon on a foggy day can be descried. Can mean literally seeing something with your eyes or intellectually comprehending something that is difficult. It should not be confused with *decry*, which means to put down or disparage. Pronounced DI-SKRY.

desultory
: Casually arranged, without particular or apparent structure. Clothes strewn on a bed lie there in a desultory fashion. Couples going nowhere in particular may stroll desultorily on a warm summer night; conversations about nothing in particular may go on in a desultory way. The word has nothing to do with depression, which some think it might. Pronounced DEH-SUHL-TUH-REE.

détente
: A relaxation of tensions between nations. Popularized by Henry Kissinger, this is a great concept and a great word to use in other situations. Coke and Pepsi could end a price war by agreeing to a détente; what's the point of mutual destruction? Pronounced DAY-TAHNT.

detritus

Both a literal and figurative way of saying "debris." Empty soda cans on a beach are detritus; so are street punks who are looking for trouble. Pronounced DEH-TRY-TUS.

de trop

From the French "too much," the word means overdone or excessive in a figurative sense. Wearing too much jewelry while working in a homeless shelter would be *de trop*. Unfortunately, using the word *de trop* is probably de trop in most situations and should be accompanied by an appropriate expression of mock snobbery. Pronounce it DEH TROH.

deus ex machina

Originally in classical Greek drama, the god that came down to earth to solve a problem that couldn't be solved by any logical turn of events. It now refers to any chance event that intervenes and prevents a disaster from occurring. Sort of like a miracle, but not as good. Pronounced DAY-OOS EX MA-KEEN-AH.

devil's tattoo

A bit obscure, but poetic, way of describing a nervous hand or foot tapping. Drumming your fingers while waiting for an important phone call is a way of making the devil's tattoo. Sometimes shortened to just "tattoo."

diacritical   A somewhat scientific way of saying "distinctive." One of the diacritical differences between a bird and an octopus is that a bird has two legs and an octopus has eight arms. It's pronounced *DYE-A-KRIT-I-KLE*.

diaphanous   Usually used to describe fabric, the word means sheer, delicate and flowing. Some sexy nightgowns are diaphanous, as are angel's wings and nylon curtains. Pronounced *DIE-AFF-AH-NUSS*.

diatribe   A bitter criticism or denunciation; an abusive dispute. Say *DIE-UH-TRYBE*. (See also *polemic*.)

dieresis   The two dots placed on top of the second of two vowels that indicates that they are supposed to be pronounced separately, as in coöperate. It's pronounced *DYE-ER-IH-SIS*.

diglot   Someone who is fluent in two languages is diglot. Can be both an adjective and a noun; it's just a different way of saying bilingual. Polyglot is the next step up. Pronounced *DYE-GLOT*.

dilatory

Moving slowly and causing delay. A turtle moves in a dilatory way. The word has nothing to do with *dilating*, which is what your eye doctor does to your pupils, or *depilatory*, which is a fancy way to say Nair. Pronounced *DILL-AH-TOR-EE*.

dilettante

A person with a superficial interest in art or any branch of knowledge; a dabbler. A dilettante is a person who doesn't hold a job and spends the days browsing through museums, taking art classes, renting old movies and cooking meals with exotic ingredients. Say *DILL-EH-TAHNT*.

dingbat

Though Archie Bunker used this word as a form of playful insult, the word really means a piece of ornamental border, such as a trim of contrasting wallpaper or a decorative piece of type. Calling someone a dingbat is tantamount to calling them a bit of decoration.

diphthong

No, it's not a type of sandal. It's a syllable containing two letters used to make a single sound. For example the *ou* in sound. Pronounced *DIF-THONG*, not *DIP-THONG*.

discreet

Not to be confused with *discrete*, which is pronounced the same way but spelled differently. Dis*creet* means being careful about what you say and the way you act, good at keeping other people's secrets; dis*crete* means separate or distinct. If you are discreet, you do not talk about your neighbor's affairs. Grains of flour are not discrete—you can't eat just one—but dinner rolls are.

disingenuous

Pretending to be innocent or naive, which has the effect of being insincere. Smiling when you've been caught with your hand in the cookie jar. Has nothing to do with ingenious, by the way. It's pronounced DIS-EN-*JEN*-YOU-US.

dissemble

Not the opposite of assemble. To give a false or misleading appearance to something. To lie. Many investigative reporters enjoy asking tough questions to crooked businesspeople and watching them squirm and dissemble.

dissimulate

A little more subtle than outright lying, it means to pretend that something is other than it is. If the attorney general asks, "Did your company dump this toxic waste?" the lying CEO would say, "No." The dissimulating CEO would say, "What waste?"

dithyramb
A wild and emotional outpouring in speech, song or writing. Naughty children provoke dithyrambs from their mothers. The tragic portions of operas are dithyrambs, too. It's pronounced *DITH-EH-RAM*.

docent
A museum guide; the person who walks you through the antiquities room in a museum and explains how Egyptians built pyramids. Pronounced *DOE-SENT*.

dotard
An old, feeble-minded person is a dotard. Almost certainly no longer politically correct, the word should be used with great care. Pronounce it *DOE-TARD*.

doughty
Hearty, brave and courageous (as distinguished from dowdy, which means plain or unattractive). Pronounced *DOWT-EE*.

doyen
The leader or commander; a *doyenne* if it's a woman. A successful artist might become the doyenne of the art world and then, if she's hip enough, the doyenne of the social world. It's pronounced *DOI-EN*.

draconian

Drastic; harsh; inhuman. Cutting off the fingers of pickpockets is considered by many to be draconian punishment. It dramatically cuts down on recidivism, however. (See also *recidivate*.) It's pronounced DRAH-COH-NEE-AN.

dragoon

To force or coerce. Not a form of pirate money, which was *dubloons*. Pirates must have dragooned their victims to get their dubloons.

dulcet

Pleasant; melodious; sweet to the eye or ear. Usually used in conjunction with the word "tone." A nightingale sings in dulcet tones. (See also *mellifluous*.) Pronounce the word DULL-SET.

dystopia

The opposite of a utopia; a place where everything goes wrong. Say it DISS-TOH-PEE-AH.

E

ecce homo
The words of Pilate when presenting Christ to his accusers, the phrase means "Behold the man—here he is." It has come to be used for any vaguely similar contemporary circumstances. A scruffy freshman comes home from college with a sack full of dirty laundry and announces sarcastically, "Ecce homo." Pronounced *ECK-AY HOE-MOE*.

echolalia
The involuntary repeating of someone's words or syllables right after they are uttered; a human echo chamber. Often associated with autism. Pronounced *ECK-OH-LAY-LEE-UH*.

ecru
Cream-colored. A little more tan than off-white, but a lot lighter than beige. Lace curtains are often ecru. Pronounced *AY-CREW* or *EH-CREW*.

ectomorphic   Literally means "skinny," but the word more accurately describes a personality type. Abbott was the ectomorph, Costello was the endomorph. Ectomorphs are generally considered type-A personalities.

ecumenical   Though it has religious implications and is often associated with the Christian church, the word is used to mean "worldwide" or "universal." An ecumenical council on hunger would deal with the problem of hunger around the globe. Pronounced *EHK-YOU-MEN-IH-CAL*.

edacious   Devouring or consuming. Someone with an edacious appetite for books reads all the time; someone with an edacious appetite for food is probably fat. Don't confuse with *audacious*, which means having chutzpah. Pronounced *ID-AY-SHUSS*.

effete   Various meanings include sterile and depleted, but the most common usage conveys decadent, fey or affected. An effete snob is someone who shuns anything remotely commonplace; an effete person indulges in rare or obscure pleasures. Pronounced *EH-FEET*.

efficacious   Efficient; effective. It might take a little longer to do a job efficaciously, but the desired effect is perfectly obtained. Ideal when used to describe medical treatment. Pronounced *EFF-EH-KAY-SHUSS*.

effluence   A flowing out or streaming forth. The waste that comes from sewage-treatment plants is effluence. "An effluence of people poured from the stadium when the ball game was over, creating quite a traffic jam." Sounds like *affluence* with an *eh* at the beginning: pronounced *EF-LOO-ENCE*.

effluvium   A bad smell, usually invisible, often associated with waste-treatment facilities. Bad breath qualifies as effluvium. The smell of apple pie does not. Say *EH-FLU-VEE-UM*.

effulge   To shine brightly, both literally and figuratively. A child's face effulges at the sight of a toy store; the surface of a lake is effulgent in brilliant sunshine.

egregious — Originally meaning just plain "exceptional," egregious has come to mean not just bad, but outstandingly bad. When things are worse than awful, they are egregious. An egregious error would be calling your present lover by an old lover's name. Beating child for bad behavior is egregious punishment. Pronounced EH-GREE-JUSS.

élan — Dash or real style; charisma plus skill. David Niven had élan. Pronounced AY-LAN.

eldritch — Weird, eerie. "His eldritch neighbor continued to leave voodoo dolls all over his front lawn." A good way for little boys to describe their little sisters.

eleemosynary — Charitable or supported by a charity. The United Way is an eleemosynary institution. Often used in legalese to distinguish from "for-profit." Pronounced ELL-EH-MAH-SINN-AR-EE.

elephantine — Like an elephant, not in size but in demeanor; lumbering and clumsy.

embracery — An effort to change someone's opinion, a judge or jury in particular, by bribes or threats.

embrangle   Sounds like a combination of *embroil* and *entangle*, and that's more or less what it means—to confuse or perplex. After hearing both sides of the case, the judge's understanding of what happened was so embrangled that she couldn't decide who was guilty.

emeritus   No longer actively employed, but kept on the staff as an honor. A professor emeritus probably doesn't teach any courses but gets paid to make a guest lecture or two. Pronounced *EH-MER-IT-US*.

éminence grise   The power behind the throne—for example, in the '80s, Nancy Reagan (or even Nancy Reagan's astrologer). Literally means "gray eminence," if you care. Pronounced *AY-MEE-NANS* GREEZ.

emolument   Not a skin cream. This is the pay or profit you receive from your job, or more likely, from a political office. Sometimes used as a nice way to say "kickback." Say *EH-MAHL-YEH-MENT*.

encephalesthenia   Exhaustion due to emotional stress rather than lack of sleep or physical work. A person who deals with an impending lawsuit by taking naps constantly is probably suffering from encephalesthenia. Pronounced EN-SEF-A-LUS-THEEN-EE-A.

encomium   A eulogy that sums up the good qualities of a dead person. It's come to mean any ceremonious praise that celebrates a person dead or alive. Pronounced EN-CO-MEE-UM.

encyclical   A letter from the pope to all his bishops. It has come to be used figuratively to refer to any very important letter. The CEO of a company could send a memo to all the division heads, who might sarcastically refer to it as the boss's encyclical. Pronounced EN-SICK-LICK-AL.

endemic   Native or indigenous to a region or place. Cypress trees are endemic to the American South; muggings are endemic to large urban environments. Distinguish from *epidemic*.

enervate   Even though this word sounds as if it denotes "to excite or make nervous," it means the opposite—to weaken or take away the energy. A long and boring lecture can be very enervating, making an audience fall asleep. Pronounced *ENN-ER-VATE*.

enigma A puzzling matter that cannot be easily explained; perhaps the most famous use of the word is to describe the Mona Lisa's smile. A nice way to say that you have absolutely no idea—"It's an enigma." Say *EN-IG-MA*.

ennui From the French word for "boredom." It means indifferent; bored in a world-weary sense. The Duke of York suffered from it—too much money, not enough to do. Pronounced *AHN-WEE*.

enormity Contrary to popular belief, the word has nothing to do with size, but with horribleness or awfulness. The enormity of a situation—like starvation in Africa—describes the extent of the tragedy.

eonism A technical way of saying transvestism. A man who dresses in women's clothing and adopts feminine postures is exhibiting eonism. Pronounced *EE-ON-ISM*.

ephemera

Something lasting only a short time. Though often used to denote triviality, ephemera involves time or lifespan, not importance. An earthquake is ephemeral, as is youth. Pronounced *EH-FEM-EH-RA*.

epicene

The word has nothing to do with the center of an earthquake; that's an *epicenter*. Epicene means reflecting both male and female characteristics; androgynous. The word has also acquired a secondary meaning as effeminate or feeble. Pronounced *EPP-EH-SEEN*.

epigone

A disciple, not famous in his own right, of a famous writer. If there were a good example, he wouldn't be a proper epigone because he'd be famous. Pronounced *EPP-I-GOHNE*.

epigram

A witty little remark such as: "An apple a day keeps the doctor away." Oscar Wilde was famous for his epigrams. The quotation at the beginning of a book, which can sometimes be an epigram, is known as an *epigraph*. Also distinguish epigram from *aphorism*, which is a brief, but not necessarily witty, expression.

epiphany

The religious meaning is a Christian feast celebrated on January 6 to commemorate the appearance of Christ, but the word is also used to mean a sudden realization of the true meaning of something. The light bulb that appears over Newton's head in a cartoon demonstrates an epiphany. The light bulb in that cartoon is also an anachronism (see *anachronism*). Pronounced EH-*PIFF*-ENN-EE.

e pluribus Unum

The Latin words that comprise the official U. S. motto. They are included in every official seal of the United States, and you may also see them on dollar bills. The phrase means, "one out of the many," as in one country out of many states.

eponymous

Giving one's name to a book, a record or an organization. Lolita is the eponymous character of Vladimir Nabokov's *Lolita*. The word is frequently used in record reviews to refer to a hit single whose title is the same as the album on which it appears. Pronounced EH-*PONN*-AH-MUSS.

equable

Uniform; not differing. In an equable distribution, everyone gets the same amount. Why not say equitable? Because equitable implies fairness. The distribution might be equal, but it might not be fair. Pronounced *EHK-WA-BULL*.

equivocal Something that's equivocal has several meanings and is therefore capable of being interpreted in several ways. Answers that are equivocal are usually intentionally so; when someone doesn't want to commit himself, he would most likely give an equivocal answer. More often heard as the antonym, *u*nequivocal, meaning "leaving no doubt." Pronounced *eh-QUIV-AH-CULL*.

ergasiophobia Fear of, or aversion, to work. What Maynard G. Krebbs suffered in the Dobie Gillis show. If you're not too lazy to pronounce it, it's *EHR-GAZ-EE-OH-FOH-BEE-A*.

ersatz Artificial, a substitute for the real thing. Sweet 'n Low is ersatz sugar; margarine is ersatz butter. Formica can be ersatz marble, wood or any other number of finishes. Pronounced *AIR-SATZ*.

eruct	An extremely erudite way of saying "belch." One way to remember the word is to think of *erupt*: "After the very large meal, the man leaned back in his chair and eructed." Pronounced *EE-RUCT*.
eschew	To avoid or shun something because you find it loathsome or unbearable. One can eschew on physical grounds, as in eschewing a wool coat in July, or in terms of taste, as in eschewing displays of physical affection in front of dinner guests. It's pronounced *ESS-CHEW* (like a sneeze).
esprit de corps	A feeling of unification or commonly held beliefs or attitudes among a group of people. The phrase can be used to describe a feeling of excitement and belonging that comes from being part of a successful group. Apple Computer had it for a while; so did the Peace Corps. Pronounced *ESS-PREE DUH CORE*.
esprit d'escalier	You probably never knew that there was a word for this—a clever remark or reply that you didn't think of at the appropriate moment but thought of too late, as in "I should have said. . . " It comes from the French phrase, "up the stairs": "I didn't think of a

snappy retort to D'Artagnan until I was already up the stairs." The next time you find yourself speechless, just say, "When I come up with the esprit d'escalier, I'll give you a call." Pronounced ESS-PREE DEH-SCAHL-YAY.

étagère

One of those pieces of furniture (often referred to by pompous antiques dealers and interior decorators) that you feel too embarrassed to admit you've never heard of. It's a group of open shelves used to store knickknacks. Pronounce it AY-TAJ-AIR.

ethos

The basic characteristics of a person, group, institution or culture; not a form of anesthesia. "The ethos of '60s America was defined by TV." Pronounced EE-THOS.

eunuch

The term for the unfortunate man who's been castrated. Traditionally employed by sheiks to protect their harem from loyal servants. Now used to describe someone who *acts* as if he'd been castrated. Pronounced YOU-NICK.

euphonious	Pleasant to listen to. The word can describe words or music. It's sometimes confused with *cacophonous*, which means the opposite. Pronounced YOU-FONE-EE-US.
evanesce	The word sounds like it means "bubbly," but it really means "to fade slowly." Champagne doesn't evanesce; sunsets do. Pronounced EH-VUH-NESS.
exacerbate	To incrementally increase the irritation or annoyance of something, as in: "Scratching his poison ivy did little but exacerbate the itching." Pronounced EX-ASS-UR-BATE.
excogitate	More than just thinking about an issue, to *excogitate* is to carefully reason it out. Pronounced EX-COJ-IH-TATE.
excoriate	To peel or take the skin from. The word is generally used figuratively. You peel an apple, but you excoriate someone for screwing up. Pronounced EX-KOR-EE-ATE.

exculpate

To free from blame. Exculpation doesn't mean forgiveness; it means that you were never guilty to begin with, and now your name is cleared. Pronounced EX-*KUL-PATE*.

exigency

An unexpected set of circumstances—but not synonymous with emergency. Urgent needs or demands arising from a set of circumstances. "I will definitely not raise taxes and positively not cut Social Security. Unless, of course, an exigency arises." Pronounced EK-*SEH-JEN-SEE*.

exordium

A more precise way to describe the introduction to a speech, presentation or book. Readers (such as yourself?) often skip over the preface, but they'll certainly spend the time to read the exordium if it is clearly labeled. Pronounced EGG-*ZORD-EE-UM*.

exoteric

Appropriate for general consumption. A lovely twist on the commonly used *esoteric*. If goat cheese is esoteric, then cheddar is exoteric.

expatiate

To expand upon, as in a speech that goes on to explain the causes and symptoms of an event. (Not to be confused with people who emigrate to a foreign land, like Hemingway when he moved to Paris in the 1920s. That's *expatriate*.) Pronounced ECKS-PAY-SHEE-ATE.

expeditious

Quick and speedy in the sense of "most rapidly accomplished." An expeditious solution to feeling nauseatingly drunk is to pass out. Pronounced EKS-PEH-DISH-USS.

extirpate

To uproot or completely destroy. An earthquake may extirpate a small village.

F

fabulist

A liar. If you want to accuse someone of not telling you the truth without instantaneously enraging them, call them a fabulist. It sounds gentler. Pronounced *FAB-YOU-LIST*.

facetious

Flippant. When a tourist asks, "How do you get to Carnegie Hall?" the facetious New Yorker answers, "Practice, practice, practice." Say *FASS-EE-SHUSS*.

facinorous

Exceptionally evil or wicked. Not just the Witch of the West; more along the lines of Satan. It's pronounced *FASS-IN-OR-US*.

fakir

An Arabic word for a guy who makes his living charming snakes or lying on a bed of nails. Not pronounced like *faker*, which might be appropriate— instead, say *FEH-KEER*.

farinaceous

Made from flour or meal and containing a lot of starch, such as bread, pasta or cereal. Vegetarians frequently eat farinaceous meals. Pronounced FARRAH-NAY-SHUS.

farrago

Not a dance—that's a *fandango*. A farrago is a jumbled hodgepodge, a mixture. If you haven't cleaned your closet in years, it's likely to be filled with a farrago of old winter coats, dirty socks, deflated balls and lonesome single shoes. Pronounced FAH-RAH-GO.

fastuous

Overbearingly snotty, pretentious, or arrogant. Not to be confused with fatuous (see *fatuous*), although fastuous people can be fatuous. Be kind to the fastuous among us, because they certainly suffer from low self-esteem. Pronounced FAST-CHOO-US.

fatuous

Foolish or inane. Clowns aren't fatuous, they're silly. A boorish drunk or a fawning suitor can easily become fatuous, however. Say FATCH-OO-US.

faux pas

From the French for "false step." This is a wonderful word for a social blunder, an error of etiquette. If you pronounce your boss's name incorrectly while introducing his speech at a large convention, you have committed a faux pas. Say *FOH PAH*.

feral

Animalistic; existing in a wild state. With his ripped shirt and slight drool, Robert seemed almost feral. Pronounced *FEER-AL* or *FEHR-AL*.

filtrum

That little canal that leads from your nose to your mouth. You knew there was a name for it, and now you know what it is.

flaccid

Limp or flabby, like the stems of wilted flowers or the thighs of people who eat too much and don't exercise. The preferred pronunciation is *FLAK-SID*, although most people say *FLASS-ID*.

flâneur

A word that comes from the French and means "idler" or "loafer," such as someone who sits around all day eating croissants and smoking Gauloises and not doing much of anything else. Not the ideal mate. It's pronounced *FLA-NYUR*.

fletcher
: A person who makes arrows. There's not much use for this word today, but you never know when you might run into Robin Hood and need some ammunition.

florid
: The word has two equally used meanings: "rosy or ruddy" and also "flowery or elaborate." The man with the florid complexion sitting behind the bar composed a poem in florid language about the woman he loves. Pronounced *FLOOR-ID*.

floromancy
: The belief that flowers have feelings and will respond to the way they are treated. People who talk to their plants and play music for them to help them grow most certainly believe in floromancy.

flotsam
: Flotsam is the floating remains of a sunken or wrecked ship. *Jetsam* is the floating stuff purposely thrown overboard to keep a ship from sinking in the first place. In our modern age, the two words are generally used together, as in, "This antique store carries a collection of the flotsam and jetsam of our society."

flout
To mock or show contempt: "The student flouted university rules by coming to class naked to the waist." It is important to distinguish *flout* from *flaunt*. Flaunt is slightly more positive. You can flaunt wealth by wearing a diamond bracelet to play tennis, for example. *Flout* rhymes with *doubt*.

flubdub
You could also say claptrap, or bunkum. But there are times when only *flubdub* is adequate to describe a ridiculous, poorly-thought-out, bombastic argument.

flump
To drop with a heavy thud. Sort of the noise you make when you collapse in a chair or throw the laundry on the bed. Talk about onomatopoeia (see *onomatopoeia*)!

foozle
To bungle or goof up. Not recommended in referring to truly serious goof-ups, like erasing your hard disk. Better for describing the acts of a waiter who brings every single person the wrong dish at dinner. It's one of those words that makes you smile every time you use it. Rhymes with *boozle*.

foray   An attack or raid. Though the word has a military connotation, it is often used metaphorically. One can make a foray into astrophysics by buying a basic text and trying to understand the principles.

forte   Has two meanings, though only one appears in everyday conversation. In classical music, forte means "play this loudly!" It's pronounced *FOUR-TAY* since the word comes from the Italian. However, the usual meaning of forte is "strong point" as in, "Bad decisions are his forte" or "Cooking Cajun food is my forte." But if you want to sound smart, be sure to say the word correctly. It's pronounced *fort* with no vowel sound on the end.

fortuitous   Depending on luck or chance; accidental. Fortuitous circumstances may help you to win some money, but they can also cause you to lose a bet. Don't use the word to convey only good luck—it describes things that are up to chance, good or bad. The correct pronunciation is *FOR-TOO-IT-US*.

founder   To be wrecked and to sink. Mostly it's ships that founder, but you could use the word figuratively.

Many people foundered in the stock market on Black Monday, for example. The word is often confused with *flounder*, which in addition to being a fish, means "to move clumsily."

fractious   Irritable, whiny, quarrelsome and rebellious, a word that best applies to the behavior of children or to adults who are acting like children. Pronounced *FRACK-SHISS*.

frisson   A shiver, as from a thrill or a fright. A frisson passes through an audience watching the shower scene in Alfred Hitchcock's *Psycho*. The word is best used as a reaction to situations that intend to scare, such as roller coaster rides or horror films. It's actually a nice way to say goosebumps. Pronounced *FREE-SON*.

fulgent   Very bright; shining or radiant. A good word for describing things like the spaceship in *Close Encounters of the Third Kind*, or the full moon. Pronounced *FUL-JENT*.

fulsome   The word originally meant "disgustingly excessive" or "copious." It has evolved to connote disgusting, tasteless and generally repellent. It's often confused to mean the opposite. A fulsome beauty exceeds the bounds of moderation and is probably not pretty at all. It's a good word to use when you want to insult someone covertly.

fungible

Easily interchangeable with something else; the opposite of unique. One loaf of bread is fungible with another. In a recession, some employers find certain employees fungible. It's pronounced *FUN-JI-BLE*.

G

gaffe
: A social blunder, just like a faux pas (see *faux pas*). If you meet the president and call him Your Royal Highness, that's a gaffe. Pronounced GAFF.

gainsay
: To contradict what another person says, as in: "I gainsay your insistence that she is brilliant; in fact, I don't find her smart at all."

galactoid
: This is a nice word because the word has nothing to do with outer space—it means "milk-like." The only overlap in the intended and misused meanings then would be the Milky Way. Coffee creamers are galactoid. So is the blood of many insects.

garrulous
: Excessively talkative in a silly, chattering way. Often misused to mean just plain friendly and willing to talk, which is *loquacious*. Save *garrulous* to describe

relatives who call frequently and make it impossible to get off the telephone no matter how hard you try. Pronounced GAH-*RUH-LUSS*.

gatefold This is a large page, folded and bound into a book or magazine. Examples are those expensive car or perfume advertisements in magazines or, most frequently, the maps included in certain books. The centerfold in *Playboy* is, as it sounds, a centrally located gatefold.

gelid A word for icy or frozen. It is rarely used figuratively. A haughty woman might have an icy stare, but gelid should be reserved for lakes in the winter or desserts offered by street vendors in the summer. Pronounce it JELL-*ID*.

genre Category. Similar items belong to the same genre. Science fiction is a genre of literature. Don't say GEN-*REH*; the word's pronounced ZHEAN-*RAH* (that's *zhean* as in Captain *Jean*–Luc Picard).

germane Another way of saying relevant, pertinent or appropriate, but strictly reserved for referring to ideas. You couldn't say that wearing a certain pair of shoes is germane to a particular set of clothes. The topic of sexual harassment is germane to a discussion about rights in the workplace, however. In a conversation about classical music, James Brown is probably not germane. Pronounced JERM-*AIN*.

gerrymander
The reorganization of the electoral districts of a state to give one political party an advantage. (Either you need this word or you don't.) Pronounced *JER*-RY-MAN-DER.

gestalt
The word comes from a school of psychology, but has come to mean a way of describing the big picture of a situation. Add together all the pieces and sum them up in a feeling. This feeling can range from the complicated way our brain solves problems to the combination of smells, feelings and sensations you get during a massage. Pronounced GEH-*SHTALT*.

gild
To coat with gold. When used figuratively, as in "gilding the lily," gild means adding refinement or ornamentation to something that doesn't need it. Pronounced like *guild*.

gimme caps   The ubiquitous baseball-style caps that bear various logos in front are called gimme caps. The word is said to come from farmers who are fond of asking tractor salesmen wearing these caps with their company name, "Gimme one of those caps."

glean   To gather or absorb information. You can glean information on nuclear weapons by reading secret plans, or glean a bit about an executive's personality by the way she shakes hands. Rhymes with *clean*.

gobbet   Another way of saying morsel or lump, as in: "Please put a gobbet of whipped cream on top of my pecan pie." Say GOB-*BIT*.

googol   The number 1, followed by 100 zeros. This is the biggest number with a name (not counting the googolplex, which is cheating). It might be nice to offer someone you love a googol kisses.

Gordian knot   An apparently unsolvable problem. Alexander (before he was *the Great*) was presented with a rope containing a huge knot, and told that the first man to untie it would rule Europe. He took out his sword and cut it in half. The word is commonly used to describe any complex problem begging for a drastic solution.

gossamer	Originally a cobweb, now the word describes any translucent, wispy object. The *Gossamer Albatross* was the first pedal-powered aircraft—so named because of its fragile gossamer wings. Pronounced GOSS-*AH-MURR*.
gracile	Slender and graceful, such as a fawn, a gazelle or a ballet dancer. It's pronounced GRASS-*ILL*.
grammalogue	This is the word for any sign or letter which signifies a word, such as & (and), $ (dollars) or @ (at). Say GRAM-*AH-LOG*.
grand guignol	Connoting a drama with strains of horror. It's the kind of word people like to use metaphorically. A difficult divorce or the cruel way someone was fired from a job might be described as a *grand guignol*. Pronounced GRAND *GEEN-YOL*.

gregarious Friendly. Occasionally used to imply insincerity, gregarious should be reserved for those that are truly outgoing and friendly. Rhymes with *precarious*.

griffin A mythical beast with the body of a lion and the head and wings of an eagle. Not the sort of animal you'd want to see flying over your Miata if the top were down.

grimalkin It sounds like some form of medieval clothing, perhaps a vest for holding arrows, but it means an old female cat. A nice way to affectionately refer to one's pet. Pronounced GRIM-*ALL*-KEN.

grommet A small, metal-reinforced hole, especially in a sail or other piece of canvas. Used to attach ropes or other tie-downs.

grum Like it sounds: grim, glum or surly. It's got a nice undertone of grumpy that comes across with the pronunciation. If your car breaks down on the third lap of the Indy 500, you have the right to act grum.

gudgeon An easy mark, someone who is duped without effort. The guys who play three-card monte on the street are just waiting for a gudgeon to come along so they can beat him and make a quick twenty bucks. Though the word sounds a bit archaic, it has a nice lumbering sound. Also a metal pivot—see *pintle*.

gullible

Often misused, this isn't really a word. It's not in the dictionary. (Got ya'! Sorry, but we couldn't resist!)

gunkhole

Though it sounds like a noun, this word is really a verb which means to sail slowly along a coastline, stopping along the way in quiet ports. To gunkhole down the East Coast to the Florida Keys would make a very relaxing vacation, provided you're not the type who gets seasick.

gunwale

The top of the side of a boat (where the rail might be). Especially used in referring to small boats such as canoes. Originally used to describe the place where you'd rest your gun (probably for shooting fish, or some other sporting activity). Pronounced *GUN-ELL*.

gustatory

Tasting. A gustatory menu in a fancy restaurant allows you to try lots of different dishes. Say *GUS-TAH-TOR-EE*.

gynarchy

Government by a woman or by women. Not to be confused with *matriarchy*, which refers to a family or tribe headed by women. Until recently, Great Britain was a gynarchy. Ironically, pronounced *GUY-NARK-EE*.

H

hajj

A pilgrimage to Mecca made at least once by pious Muslims. Can be used figuratively to refer to any pilgrimage. Many senior citizens make their annual hajj to Florida in the winter, for example. Pronounced *HAHJ*.

halcyon

The word derives from an ancient fabled bird that bred during the winter solstice and charmed the winds and seas, calming them during that period. It has simply come to mean calm, tranquil, and happy. People often refer to "the halcyon days" when they are feeling nostalgic about an easier or more prosperous time in their lives. It's pronounced *HAL-SEE-ON*.

halidom

A holy place, thing, or sanctuary, such as a chapel or church. Halidome can also be spelled with an *e* on the end, and it's pronounced *HAL-IH-DOME*.

handsel   Not Gretel's brother; there's no *d* in his name. A gift
           or present that is meant to bring good luck, such as a
           bottle of champagne to the owner of a new restau-
           rant. Pronounced *HAND-SELL*.

harbinger A person, thing or event that foreshadows the arrival
           of something. The first robin is a harbinger of spring;
           the sight of billboards for hundreds of miles is a
           harbinger of Wall Drug in South Dakota. It's pro-
           nounced *HAR-BIN-JER*, not *HAR-BING-ER*.

harridan   A bad-tempered old woman; a hag. *Harridan* could be
           used to describe your eighth-grade history teacher, a
           nasty neighbor or the wicked witch in a fairy tale.
           Pronounced *HA-RIH-DEN*.

haruspex   In ancient Rome, a fortuneteller who predicted the
           future by reading sheep entrails. What a great word to
           describe a trend analyst who doesn't know what he's
           talking about.

havelock   A cloth covering for a cap which has a flap to protect
           the back of the neck from the sun—the kind of thing
           Lawrence of Arabia wore. Players on outdoor urban

basketball courts wear havelocks today. Pronounced *HAVE-LOK*.

hedonist A person addicted to things that give pleasure or happiness. A hedonist puts chocolate ice cream *and* hot fudge on a flourless chocolate cake, or spends class time sunbathing while attending the University of Miami. Pronounced *HE-DUN-IST*.

hegemony This word frequently crops up in academic texts, and means political and/or economic leadership, as in one country over another or one state over another. Japan has hegemony over the United States in the consumer electronics industry. Pronounced *HEH-JEM-EN-EE*.

hegira A flight or escape from one situation to another that offers better circumstances. It often refers to the flight of Mohammed from Mecca to Medina in 622 A.D., but it may be used metaphorically, as in making a hegira to a job that provides better pay and more interesting work. Say *HE-JIH-RA*.

hermaphrodite

This is a human being or an animal that has both male and female sex organs. Do not confuse with an *androgyne*, someone who exhibits both male and female sexual manners and traits. There are many androgynous people in the world, but very few hermaphrodites.

heterodox

A person or a belief that is not in accordance with established orthodox belief. Heterodox is generally used to refer to religion but can be used more broadly. For example, a Catholic who maintains heterodox beliefs may support the abortion movement. A professor at a conservative university who has heterodox ideas may cancel all classes in favor of life experience internships and private conferences. Pronounced *HETT-ERR-OH-DOX*.

heteronym

A word spelled like another, but with a different sound and meaning, such as *lead* and *lead*, *read* and *read*. Pronounced *HET-ERR-OH-NIM*.

heuristic

The hints, techniques and concepts we use to make decisions. How does a doctor decide what drug to prescribe? Why did you pick a blue shirt instead of a red one? An important concept, because understanding the heuristics that we use to make a decision can help us learn how to do it better. Pronounced HYUR-ISS-TIC.

hiatus A break in a career or routine. Optimistic TV producers talk about a show going on hiatus, when they really mean that it has been canceled. Pronounce it HI-AY-TUSS. (See also *lacuna.*)

highbinder This is a word for swindler or confidence man. It's a particularly nice word because you can accuse someone of being a highbinder without insulting him—he probably won't know what the word means! (See also *gudgeon.*)

hirsute Hairy. A man in need of a shave is hirsute. You would not describe a sticky or hairy situation as hirsute. Pronounced HEER-SUIT.

histrionic Overly dramatic; so excessively theatrical as to be unbelievable. A teenager who sobbingly declares that he will die if he is cut from the tennis team is engaging in histrionics. Pronounced HISS-TREE-ON-IC.

hoary
Gray- or white-haired with age. There is no insult in this word. Old Man Time has a hoary beard. Santa Claus does, too. Rhymes with *story*.

Hobson's choice
Thomas Hobson was not a philosopher, but a 16th-17th century English stable owner who insisted that his clients take the horse closest to the door. The phrase, named after Hobson, means a decision that offers no alternative. In short—take it or leave it.

hoi polloi
People often use this word to mean the fancy people in a society, but it means the opposite. The hoi polloi are the common people, the vulgar masses whom Marie Antoinette dismissed by suggesting that they eat cake. It's pronounced HOY POLL-OY.

homeopathy
Though the word has come to be used to mean natural medicine, such as ginseng or flower therapy, as opposed to pharmaceuticals, it means treating disease by administering minute doses of drugs that normally produce symptoms like those of the disease. Pronounced HOE-MEE-OP-UH-THEE.

homily

A sermon or a moral lecture. Priests deliver homilies on living morally; coaches deliver homilies on living cleanly; parents often deliver homilies on both. Pronounced *HOM-ILL-EE*.

homunculus

Literally meaning "little man," this word can be used to refer to anybody who's more than 20 years old and less than five feet tall, but the word is more commonly used figuratively to mean "the little man inside the box making decisions." Often used in philosophy as a slick way to describe consciousness or computers. Your mind is nothing more than a skull with a homunculus inside, making the decisions (who's inside the homunculus? another homunculus!). Pronounced *HO-MUNG-KYUH-LUSS*.

honorarium

A token payment made for professional services, generally less than should be charged. When a congressman gives a speech, the conference organizers don't degrade him by paying him—they give him an honorarium.

hoodoo

A nice folksy way of saying bad luck; kind of like voodoo with a vengeance. He suffered a bolt of hoodoo last month when he lost his job, cracked up his car, *and* misplaced his dry-cleaning ticket.

hortatory
: Urging someone to do something. The sergeant made a hortatory speech in an effort to convince the boys to join the army. Pronounced *HOR-TAH-TOR-EE*.

hot spur
: A rash, impetuous person who is volatile, hot-tempered, and easily spurred to violence. There's some generosity in the insult; it's kinder than calling someone a homicidal maniac.

hubris
: Excessive pride; proud to a fault. Originally used to describe the flaw of mere mortals who challenged the gods. Icarus was guilty of hubris, as is Donald Trump. Pronounced *HYOU-BRISS*.

huggermugger
: Chaotic secrecy. The machinations of the CIA or the behind-closed-doors board meetings of corporations under siege are best described as huggermugger. Obsession with confidentiality masks the total lack of control, insight or understanding demonstrated by the participants.

hunks

Not beefcake, like a male model—that's a *hunk*. A mean, disagreeable, old person who is often cheap and miserly. Scrooge was a hunks before he met his ghosts.

hyperbole

An intentionally exaggerated exaggeration, not meant to be taken literally. "You're the nicest person I've ever met" might be an exaggeration, but "You're the nicest person in the whole wide world" is a hyperbole. Pronounced HIGH-*PER*-BO-LEE.

hypocorism

A word for baby talk like "kitchee, kitchee, koo," or for pet names like "Snookeeookums," "Sweetie pie" or "My little dumpling." Newlyweds and parents of newborn babies are fond of speaking in hypocorisms —before they know better. It's pronounced HI-POCK-ER-ISM.

I

iatrogenic

The sad situation of getting sicker after treatment by a doctor. Lately expanded to connote making anything worse in an effort to make it better. Someone who goes into a hospital to be treated for a broken leg and then catches a bad virus from the person in the neighboring bed suffers from the iatrogenic conditions common to many hospitals. Pronounced *EE-YAT-RUH-JEN-IC*.

ichthyoid

This is a scientific word for "fish-like." Some underwater creatures are ichthyoid; so are the handshakes of certain disagreeable people. Pronounced *ICK-THEE-OID*.

iconoclast

Someone who attacks traditional or popular values, beliefs or symbols of traditional values. The man carrying the "God is Dead" sign is an iconoclast, as is a politician who attacks beloved TV stars. Along with hubris (see *hubris*), this word belongs in your everyday vocabulary. Pronounced EYE-CON-OH-CLAST.

iconography   Pictorial or symbolic representation of something. Cave writings depict ancient cultures by telling stories through pictures; in the same way, urban graffiti often provides the iconography for contemporary urban street culture. Pronounced EYE-KON-AH-GRAFF-EE.

idem   The Latin word for "ditto." (Not those blue-printed papers you used to sniff in elementary school.) Ditto means "repeat that last item again." Some people prefer to use *idem* rather than *ditto*, abbreviated to *id.* in scholarly works. It's pronounced EYE-DEM or EE-DEM.

idiogamist   A man who is capable of engaging in sexual intercourse only with his wife. Pronounce it ID-EE-AH-GAM-IST.

idioglossia
: This is the word for the invented, unintelligible form of speech shared by twins, siblings or any children who are closely associated. You could probably extend the definition to describe intense technical discussions between computer whizzes, or the short-hand used by waiters at a short-order lunch counter. It's pronounced ID-EE-A-*GLOSS*-EE-A.

idiograph
: This is not the writing of a stupid person, but rather the word for any private trademark or signature. A common idiograph among teenage girls is to dot the i's in their names with a heart. Pronounced IH-DEE-OH-GRAFF. (See also *paraph*.)

ignoble
: It basically means the opposite of "noble"—mean, contemptible and of generally low character. Taking credit for someone else's work is an ignoble act, as is lying, stealing, cheating and generally acting like a selfish, ungenerous jerk. Say it IG-*NO*-BULL.

imbroglio
: A state of confusion; an entangled mess. Often used to describe a mob of players duking it out at home plate, or a skirmish among many factions on Capitol Hill. The correct pronunciation is IM-*BROHL*-YOH (don't pronounce the *g*).

imminent — About to happen. Thunderstorms and temper tantrums are often described as imminent. *Imminently* is a powerful way to say "soon."

impecunious — Poor. The word has a slightly antiquated flavor. Huckleberry Finn was impecunious; the people on welfare lines today are unemployed and poor. Pronounced IM-PECK-*YOO*-NEE-US.

implacable — Not to be pleased, convinced or reconciled. Implacable carries with it more class than *stubborn*. Say it IM-*PLACK*-AH-BULL.

importune — To beg or plead with great intensity and persistence. A child might beg her mother to let her stay up late; a man might importune his wife not to leave him. Choose *importune* when the importance of the plea is great enough to merit the word. Say IM-POOR-*TUNE*.

imprimatur — A stamp of approval from an acknowledged expert. An endorsement in the form of a logo, signature or brand name. Jack Nicklaus lends his imprimatur to a line of golf clubs. He didn't design them, he doesn't make them and he doesn't play with them; he just endorses them with his name. Pronounce it *IM-PREH-MAH-TER*.

impunity   Freedom from punishment. If you do something with impunity, you know you'll get away with it; if you do it without impunity, you know you'll be in deep trouble—and you're not using the word correctly either! Say *IM-PEW-NIT-EE*.

inchoate   Not yet formed; just begun. A novel is inchoate after the first chapter has been written; the earth was inchoate when nothing existed but primordial ooze. Pronounced *IN-KOH-IT*.

incubus   An evil spirit that annoys people while they are sleeping and, in particular, a spirit that badgers women for sexual favors. A better way to say you didn't have a very good night's sleep. Pronounced *IN-CUBE-US*.

inculpate   The opposite of exculpate; to blame, more in a legal sense than a moral one. Thieves and murderers are inculpated by society; parents are blamed when their children misbehave. Don't confuse the word with *inculcate,* which means to teach by constant repetition. Pronounced *IN-CULL-PAYT*.

indefectible

Perfect; without flaw or defect. It can be used to describe a person's character, as well as a perfect diamond or a work of art. Pronounced *IN-DEE-FECT-I-BLE*.

indemnity

Insurance or compensation against loss. You can indemnify someone against damages that may occur because of your actions. For movie buffs, double indemnity is an insurance phrase for a double pay-off in certain instances—murder, for example.

ineffable

Indescribable, impossible to capture in words. Usually used for things that are indescribably good or too mysterious or spiritual to put into words. A Mounds bar is not ineffable, but the beauty of nature may be.

in extremis

The Latin expression for "near death." When a person on his deathbed makes a sudden decision, such as to change his will and leave everything to a distant cousin, his decision is said to have been made in extremis. The word is often misused to mean a state of near insanity, since things that are decided in extremis are by their very nature, well, extreme. Pronounced IN EX-*STREEM*-ISS.

in flagrante delicto An evocative Latin phrase for being caught in the middle of a sexual act. A wife leaves work early and comes home to find her husband *in flagrante delicto* with another woman. (Sexual infidelity must have been common in Roman times, too.) Pronounce it IN FLAG-*RAN*-TAY DEL-*IK*-TOE.

infamous This doesn't mean "not famous." Infamous describes a famous person whose fame is based on unsavory acts. Serial killers and hardened criminals are infamous, as are most dictators. Pronounced IN-*FEH*-MUSS.

inflammable Just like flammable, but the word is longer. Both types of objects will burst into flames when lit. No one really knows the difference.

ingenue A naive young woman or, just as common, an actress who plays the role of a naive young woman. Marilyn Monroe made the type famous. It's pronounced EN-*JEN*-OO.

ingenuous

Not *ingenious*, nor *disingenuous*. Ingenuous means naive and unworldly. (Ingenious means clever. Disingenuous means *pretending* to be innocent and naive.) "His big brown eyes and charming, ingenuous grin made him very likeable." Pronounce it IN-*JENN*-YOU-US.

inimical

Often confused with *inimitable* (which means impossible to imitate), inimical means hostile and unfriendly. An inimical rival should be avoided, not because he's in a class by himself but because he's downright vicious.

iniquity

Complete wickedness; often found in a den for some reason. Say IH-*NICK*-WIHT-EE.

innervate

The opposite of enervate, which means to weaken or drain. Innervate means to stimulate or furnish with nervous energy. Some things can be enervating *and* innervating at the same time, such as spending several hours with a group of raucous kids. Pronounced INN-ERV-ATE.

inscrutable

Mysterious; difficult to understand or fully grasp. A great catch-all word that can be applied to people, ideas, written works or life in general. Obscure philosophers are inscrutable; shy people who don't talk much are often inscrutable.

insouciance   Indifference, but with a subtle twist of devil-may-care. An apathetic person may be simply indifferent to what's going on; a person who intentionally acts as if she doesn't care in order to look cool or invulnerable is showing insouciance. Pronounced *IN-SOO-SEE-ENTS*.

intents and purposes   Usually used in the phrase "for all intents and purposes," it means under usual circumstances or during normal conditions: For all intents and purposes, a seat belt increases the safety of the driver. Not *intensive purposes,* a common mistake.

interdict   To forbid or sternly prohibit. It's best used with official pronouncements. A key word in the war against drugs, usually accomplished by the Coast Guard. Pronounced *IN-TER-DIKT* (not *IN-TER-DITE.*)

interjacent   In between, unlike *adjacent,* which means next to. Most often used in mathematical discussions, but can be applied in everyday speech, as in: "They took a hotel room that was interjacent to the rooms of their friends so they could intercede if a fight broke out."

internecine

Since the word is almost always used in conjunction with "warfare," it has come to be misunderstood to mean "nuclear." In fact, it means "mutually destructive." A divorce can be internecine, so can squabbling among divisions of a company. Pronounced *IN-TER-NESS-EEN*.

intestate

Dying without a will. In many states, this costs your heirs lots of money. For some reason, many Americans believe that creating a will somehow encourages an early visit from the Grim Reaper.

intort

Kind of like contort, but neater. When you twist or curl something around a fixed point, you intort it. Pretzels could be described this way, complicated logic probably not.

intractable

Stubborn or obstinate, such as a child who won't behave even after being scolded.

intransigent

Like *intractable* (see above) but with more intensity, the word means stubborn, obstinate, refusing to compromise or change an opinion or belief. It implies a bit of ideological commitment that adds to the refusal to change, as in: "The employees demonstrated in front of the building to demand better working conditions, but the management remained intransigent." It's pronounced *IN-TRANS-IH-JENT*.

inure

To become hardened and unaffected by hardship, difficulty or attack. The boy was teased so often for being shorter than his classmates that after a while he became inured to the taunting words and tried out for the basketball team. Pronounced *IN-YOOR*.

invective

Although this word sounds as if it should be an adjective, it's a noun that means "strongly abusive verbal criticism." Ship captains are well known for using invective to motivate their sailors. Say *INN-VECK-TIVE*.

irascible

Of an irritable temperament; easily annoyed. An irascible person has no patience for anybody or anything, and flies off the handle at the slightest provocation. Often associated with cantankerous old men. It's pronounced *IR-ASS-IH-BULL*.

irenic

Peaceful, calm and capable of inducing serenity. Save this word to refer to personalities rather than things. Lakes are placid; people who meditate are said to be irenic. Pronounced *EYE-REN-IK*.

iterate

It means the same thing as reiterate: to repeat over and over. Use *reiterate* if you want people to understand what you're saying; save *iterate* for describing learning by doing something over and over again, getting better or more accurate each time. That's called an iterative process. An iteration describes *one* of the repetitions. Pronounced *IT-ER-ATE*.

J

jape
This is a nice word because it's both a noun and a verb. To joke or to tease; also a taunt, wisecrack or practical joke. "He continued to jape me over my new glasses." "I opened the door and a huge bowl of Jell-O fell on my head—quite a jape!"

jejune
This word has nothing to do with the month in which everyone gets married. It means dull and uninteresting, immature and lacking in wisdom. Adolescents are notorious for being considered jejune by adults and for considering everybody, adults included, jejune. Pronounced *ZHI-ZHOON*.

jerry-built
Held together with toothpicks and glue; shoddily built or slapped together. Very similar to *jury-rig*, which implies something built hastily with whatever was at hand. "He jury-rigged a contraption to automatically rock the cradle, but since it was jerry-built, it collapsed."

jettison   To throw overboard. Jetsam (see *flotsam*) is jettisoned all the time.

jihad   The word literally means a holy war waged by Muslims as a religious duty, but it has come to be used for any cause undertaken on behalf of certain principles. Pronounced *JIH-HAHD*.

jingoism   Aggressive patriotism, usually manifested by chanting slogans and waving banners or symbols. Jingoism has something of a negative connotation because it suggests unreasonable excess. Often associated with xenophobia (see *xenophobia*), which is the fear of foreigners.

jocose   Someone who's always joking around is jocose. Compare to *verbose*, which describes someone who's always talking. Pronounced *JOH-COSE*.

jodhpurs   Those ridiculous pants, worn by horseback riders and motorcycle cops, with very wide thighs and narrow calves. Dudley DoRight wears a pair. Named after a city in western India, in case you were curious. Pronounced *JOD-PURRS*.

joey

A baby kangaroo. Not just because his mama named him that. All baby kangaroos are called joeys, just as all baby bears are called cubs.

Jungian

Carl Jung was a contemporary and follower of Freud, and is best known for his theories of a universal mythology, a connection that brings us all back to basic roots. If you believe in this stuff, you're Jungian. Say it *YOONG-EE-UN*.

juvenescent

Youthful. It has no negative connotation like immature or naïve; it literally means "young." Plants are juvenescent in the seedling stage; the moon is juvenescent when it first begins to wax. Pronounced *JOO-VAN-ESS-ENT*.

juxtapose

This is one of those words people love to use to sound smart, particularly when criticizing art, fiction or films. The word means to put next to something else for comparison. You can juxtapose the letters on the Scrabble board to score more points.

K

Kafkaesque   A reference to the early 20th-century novels of Franz Kafka, whose surreal, nightmarish plots revolve around protagonists who are caught in a strangling web of bureaucracy. Now applied to any event in which a person is trapped by stultifying bureaucratic measures. Pronounced *KAHFF-KAH-ESK*.

kakistocracy   A wonderfully descriptive word, often needed and rarely recognized, that means "government by the worst people in the state." It's pronounced *KACK-ISS-TOCK-RAH-SEE*.

katabatic   Moving down a slope or valley. Skiing is clearly a katabatic sport. Pronounced *CAT-A-BAT-IK*.

kef   The word refers to a drowsy, dreamy state induced by a narcotic, such as marijuana, but can be used to mean a stupor brought about by anything. A dull speaker can put his audience in a kef; traveling by car on a long turnpike can do the same thing. Say *KEHF*.

kegler   It sounds like a kegler might be a person who drinks a lot of beer, but in fact it's a person who bowls, such as Ralph Kramden of "The Honeymooners." So, it may in fact be a person who drinks a lot of beer.

ken   Area of expertise or authority. "'That's outside my ken,' said the detective." Rhymes with *zen*.

kente   A type of African cloth. Developed hundreds of years ago, kente cloth is a sign of royalty and wealth. Also spelled *kinte*. Pronounced *KEHN-TAY*.

key grip   One of the unknown movie professions seen in the credits of every film. The grip sets up scenery and camera dollies; the head of all the grips on a film is called the key grip.

killjoy   The opposite of "the life of the party." Your dour friend who is always pointing out the risks, the dangers and the downsides is a killjoy. Kids call him or her a spoilsport.

kinetic

Filled with motion. Ballet is a kinetic art, and a kinesiologist studies human motion. Pronounced KIN-EH-TICK.

kiosk

A small, open-sided building, often used for selling tickets or dispensing information. It's pronounced KEE-OSK, not KY-OSK.

kismet

Fate or destiny. Usually used in a positive sense—it was kismet that Lana Turner happened to be at the counter at Schwab's the day she was discovered. Pronounced KIZ-MET.

kith

Your family is kin; your friends are kith. When the whole gang gets together, you refer to them as your kith and kin.

knell

The sound of a bell tolling. The word is most often used to refer to the sound of funeral bells ringing. Almost always coupled with "death." For instance, "Videocassettes sounded the death knell for revival movie houses." Rhymes with *bell*.

knurl

A series of small ridges, such as those found along the edge of a quarter. It's a good word to know if you need to explain any magic tricks that involve coins.

kowtow

To bow before someone. Though it can mean bowing in a gesture of genuine respect, as it did when the word was coined by the Chinese, it has come to mean groveling or currying favor. Rhymes with *how now brown cow*.

krotoscope

Remember those old dance shows on TV when prizes were awarded to the contestant who earned the most applause? The device used to measure applause is a krotoscope. Probably developed in some secret government lab. Say CROW-TEH-SCOPE.

kudos

Not a method of self-defense, or a brand of chocolate bar, but applause or praise. Critics extend kudos to playwrights. Say KOO-DOZE.

L

labile
: Although the word means unstable in general, it is most frequently used to mean emotionally unstable, as in temperamental or moody. A child who cries at the slightest provocation is labile; an adult who laughs too loudly at a joke and then sinks suddenly into depression is also labile. Labile people generally make others uncomfortable, since every reaction comes across like an overreaction. Pronounce it like *label*.

lachrymose
: Given to weeping. It has less to do with being sad than it does with shedding tears. The movies that we call tear-jerkers make us cry because they are sad. Eyedrops, air pollution or a bitter wind can make us lachrymose. Pronounced *LACK-RI-MOSE*.

lacuna
: This is not a South Sea islet, a California beach, a type of punctuation or a foreign currency. A lacuna is a rather elegant way of describing a gap or a missing

portion. The most famous lacuna of all is the 18-minute gap in the Watergate tapes. If you borrow a book from a careless friend and the middle fifty pages are missing, you might call to ask what happened in the lacuna. It's pronounced LAK-*YOO*-NAH. The plural is *lacunae*, and surprisingly enough, is pronounced LAK-*YOO*-NEE.

lambent   Dealing gently but brilliantly with a subject, or touching something lightly and playfully on the surface. Intelligent criticism of a work of art might be considered lambent; fiction dealing broadly but cleverly with society's ills is lambent. On the more literal side, a poet might describe the lambent sunlight playing on the surface of a stream.

lanai   Hotel jargon for a private terrace or balcony that comes with a room. It's a good idea when on vacation to request a LAN-*EYE*, even if you're not in Hawaii.

lanugo   All expectant parents know this one because they read the book that contains photos of a developing fetus. Lanugo is literally the soft, downy hairs that cover the fetus and newborn babies. Say LAH-*NEW*-GO.

lee

The sheltered side of something; the side away from the wind. Most things have a leeward (say *LEE-WORD* or *LOO-WURD*) side and a windward side, at least most things in windy places. Rhymes with *flee*.

legerdemain

A particularly elegant way of saying dexterity in the use of one's hands to perform magic tricks, juggling, or other feats of deception. The word might be used more wryly, as in "That creative accountant's tax work was a feat of legerdemain." Pronounced *LEJ-ER-DEM-ANE*.

leitmotif

A theme maintained throughout a body of work, particularly a musical work, associated with a character, an idea or an emotion. It's pronounced *LITE-MO-TEEF*.

lethologica

A temporary inability to remember a word or a name; the condition that makes you screw up your face and say, "Ooh...it's on the tip of my tongue." The next time a friend forgets a word, here's hoping you don't say, "Oh, there's a word for that condition. It's called...ooh...I forget." It's pronounced *LETH-AL-OH-JIK-AH*.

lexicon

This word refers to the working or usable vocabulary of a language, a person or a culture. After reading this book, your lexicon should be greatly expanded. Say *LECKS-IH-CON*.

libertarian

An advocate of liberty of thought and action. Also refers to a political party which supports minimal gov-ernment intervention, except in law and military defense.

libertine

Not to be confused with a *libertarian* (see above), a libertine is someone who advocates the liberty to be dissolute, particularly with regard to sexual needs. A libertine, like a rake or a roué (see *roué*) seeks to satisfy personal lust at just about any cost. Don Juan was a libertine.

licentious

A licentious person is a *libertine* (see above); someone uncontrolled in sexual indulgence. Say *LIE-SEN-SHUSS*.

lickerish

Lustful and lecherous. (See *licentious* above.)

light year

Definitely not a length of time. It's a distance, specifi-cally the distance light travels in one year (just over five trillion miles). Excellent for use in particularly *hyperbolic* (see *hyperbole*) sentences.

Lilliputian Describes someone from the mythical island of Lilliput. Featured in Jonathan Swift's novel *Gulliver's Travels*, these people are about three inches tall. A fancy way to say "small." (See also *yahoo*.)

limn To capture through an artistic medium; to evoke or describe, either in a drawing or in words. A poet may limn the beauty of a sunset in rhyming couplets; an artist may limn the beauty of a person or an object using clay or watercolors or shards of pottery, for that matter. Pronounced LIMM.

limpid This is one of those words you're sure you know the meaning of—droopy, limp, flaccid (see *flaccid*), right? Wrong. In fact, limpid means clear or transparent. A country stream is limpid; Elizabeth Taylor's eyes are limpid—even unpolluted air could be described as limpid.

linchpin A lot like a cotter pin. Traditionally, a piece of hardware that holds together a piece of machinery, now used to describe the crucial element in an argument or organization.

lingua franca   Sounds like a pasta dish, but it's not. The phrase describes a common language—a good way to break the ice in a difficult negotiation. When people talk sports, they are engaging in a lingua franca. Say it like it looks: *LING-WAH FRANK-AH*.

lissom   Supple; agile; lithe. Ballet dancers are lissom. Olympic athletes are lissom. Michael Jordan is lissom, even when he's just walking down the street. Sometimes spelled *lissome*. Say *LISS-UHM*.

litotes   Someone who speaks in litotes uses understatements in which two negatives make a positive. "She's not a bad actress" is a litotes; so is "You're not looking half-bad." Pronounce it *LIE-TOH-TEEZ*.

liverish   A word used to describe people who have personalities not unlike the taste of liver—if you don't like liver. A liverish person is unpleasant, disagreeable, easily irritated and generally icky to be around.

livery   The clothing or uniform worn by the servants of high-ranking people. A chauffeur's suit and cap is his livery; the crewcut, sunglasses, dark suit and white shirt is the livery of an FBI agent. The term can be used somewhat facetiously to refer to any uniform. Black leather, spiky hair and lots of earrings is the livery of the punk scene, for example. Say *LIHV-ER-EE*.

livid

The word literally means the color of flesh after being strangled—bluish-gray—but most of the time it's used to describe furious anger, as in choking with anger. If you arrive a half-hour late for a meeting with someone who hates to be kept waiting, you're likely to find that the person you are meeting is either livid or not there. Say *LIH-VID*.

logorrhea

Not a bad case of indigestion, but close. The word basically means diarrhea of the mouth. When you meet someone who makes you nervous and you begin to chatter nervously and say stupid things that you regret later, you are suffering from a temporary case of logorrhea. Things could be worse—it's a real medical condition and some people suffer it permanently. It's pronounced *LOG-A-REE-AH*.

looby   A silly, stupid person—a novel twist on *boob*.

Lothario   A reference to a character in an 18th-century play by
                   Rowe, this is a man who charms women and lies to
                   them in order to gain sexual favors, not unlike a rake,
                   a roué (see *roué*), a libertine (see *libertine*), or a
                   licentious (see *licentious*) man.

louche   Decadent, depraved, seedy and immoral. The streets
                   of Saigon during the Viet Nam war were louche;
                   certain bars along the waterfront in port cities are
                   louche. You can use the word to describe a person's
                   character, but it's better used to capture an atmos-
                   phere. Pronounced LOOSH.

loup   A half-mask, the kind that covers only the eyes and
                   nose. Batman and Catwoman favor them, although
                   theirs are clearly more elaborate than the average
                   loup. Rhymes with *soup*.

lubricious   You can pronounce it LOO-BRIK-US or LOO-BRISH-US,
                   and either way it means slippery in a literal sense (as
                   in lubricated), or slippery in a more figurative sense
                   (lecherous, lascivious or licentious). *Rakes, roués,*

Lotharios (see above) are all lubricious; so is a newly
waxed floor or a well-oiled hinge.

lucubrate

To burn the midnight oil—to work or study late into
the night. The home office and the personal computer have made lucubration far easier. Pronounced
LOO-KYEH-BRATE.

lumpen

Has nothing to do with oatmeal. Most often seen
with "proletariat," as in "lumpen proletariat." It
means people deprived of their rights and homes, or
otherwise degraded in social standing.

lurid

Vulgar; designed in a way that appeals to our baser
instincts, which generally means not very subtle.
Lurid colors are exceptionally bright; lurid clothes are
gaudy or revealing; lurid language is probably
peppered with violent or sexual references; lurid
dancing is sexually suggestive. It's not necessarily
bad, just blatant. It's pronounced *LOOR-ID*.

lysophobia

How's this for self-fulfilling prophecy? The word
means a morbid dread of going insane. It's pronounced *CRAY-ZEE*. Sorry: *LISS-O-FOE-BEE-A*.

M

macédoine
: Not a citizen of Macedonia. This is the kind of word you see on the menus of fancy restaurants that offer things like *médaillons* of beef or chicken *en croûte*. It means diced and mixed. A macédoine of fruit is nothing more or less than a fruit cocktail. But it sounds much more exotic, doesn't it? It's pronounced MASS-EH-*DWAN*.

machination
: This word really rolls off the tongue. It means a secret plot or scheme and has a particularly sneaky and underhanded tone. Competitive coworkers often get involved in machinations to move up in the office hierarchy. Pronounced MAK-IN-*AY*-SHUN.

macroeconomics
: The study of the broad and general aspects of an economy, such as the general level of inflation, rather than of a particular aspect of a society's economy (see *microeconomics*).

madrilène

Sounds like an 18th-century dance step or a pretentious name for a little girl, but it's neither. In fact, it's a kind of soup—tomato-flavored broth, served jellied and cold or liquid and hot. At least you now know whether you want to order some next time you're having a macédoine of fruit (see *macédoine*). Say MAD-*REE*-LEN.

magna cum laude

Get it straight: *summa cum laude* is the highest praise and it means just that; *magna cum laude* is the next highest and means with great praise; *cum laude* is the lowest of three honors and it means, simply, with honor. If you graduate with any of the three you're doing just great. By the way, it's pronounced MAG-*NA KUM* LOUD-*UH*.

magniloquent

If you call someone magniloquent, it's not a compliment. It means boastful, pompous, and full of hot air—a great way to insult a magniloquent person.

maillot

A type of fabric of a particularly close knit, the kind often used to make one-piece swimsuits. It's come to denote any one-piece swimsuit, regardless of the fabric. Pronounced MY-*OH*.

134

maladroit This word has several meanings, none of them complimentary. It means physically awkward or clumsy, as well as verbally awkward in the sense of tactless. Though the word comes from the French, it's been anglicized to be pronounced *MAL-AH-DROYT*.

malapropism The confusion of similar-sounding words, usually with ridiculous results. "Beware the ideas of March." "It's not the heat; it's the humility." Pronounced *MAL-AH-PROP-ISM*.

malfeasance A somewhat official form of misconduct. If a public official commits a crime while in office, he or she commits a malfeasance. The word is generally not used to refer to ordinary people; they commit crimes. Embezzling campaign funds for private use, for example, is malfeasance. It's pronounced *MAL-FEE-ZANCE*.

malice The desire to see a great deal of evil done upon another. Worse than spite or holding a grudge, malice is serious hatred. Pronounced *mahl-iss*. Rhymes with "*Alice*."

malinger

To pretend to be sick in order to avoid work. A child who doesn't want to go to school can pretend to have a sore throat. If he wants to be honest, he can tell his parents he's malingering and hope they don't know what the word means. Pronounced MA-*LING*-ER.

manqué

The word is usually combined with "artist" or "poet," as in *artist manqué*, perhaps because it means unfulfilled or might-have-been. (After all, who ever heard of an accountant manqué?) Pronounced MAN-*KAY*.

mare's-nest

Something thought to be a great discovery that is really nothing more than a big hoax is a mare's-nest. Maybe the name comes from the fact that horses can't lay eggs?

martinet

A strict disciplinarian. It has a military connotation—but it doesn't have to. General Patton was a martinet; but so was that evil history teacher who gave you too much homework every night.

matutinal

A rather economical way of saying "happening in the morning" from the French "matin." Breakfast is a matutinal meal; many people like to take matutinal walks; certain radio programs are matutinal. Pronounced MA-*TOO*-TEH-NALL.

maunder O.K. to confuse with *meander*, which means more or less the same thing. To maunder is to walk or talk in a random or confused manner. "The sick man, flushed with fever, maundered on about his wasted life."

maverick In the spirit of the famed TV sheriff, a maverick is a nonconformist or a rebel, a person whose thoughts and actions are different from most others. A maverick is willing to break ground with his beliefs. An iconoclast (see *iconoclast*) believes in attacking established beliefs, but a maverick believes in creating new ones. The Beatles were mavericks in rock and roll; Einstein was a maverick physicist.

mawkish Overly sentimental or maudlin. Your great-aunt, who is always hugging and crying and talking about who's in her will, is mawkish. It's not a good way to be. Soap operas are mawkish; so are bad movies. Say MAWK-*ISH*.

meet
There's a nice, slightly archaic, meaning for this word aside from the obvious one. Something that is meet is fitting, suitable or appropriate. Wearing a tie to certain restaurants is meet attire. Coming up with a good retort is finding meet words for the situation and avoiding an esprit d'escalier (see *esprit d'escalier*).

megrims
A depression or sinking into low spirits. Someone down in the dumps is suffering the megrims. Pronounced MEE-GRIMS.

mélange
This French word for "mixture" is slightly more evocative than plain old "mixture." It's used for more subtle descriptions. A combination of flour, sugar and milk is a mixture. A blend of passion, romance and eros is a mélange. Say MAY-LAHNJ.

mêlée
One step short of a riot; a confused or tumultuous fight among several people. Useful in painting a powerful word picture. Pronounced MAY-LAY.

mellifluous
A nightingale's song is mellifluous, as is a lover's whisper. Music or sound that flows smoothly or

sweetly, like the sound of the word itself: MELL-*IF*-LOO-*USS*.

mensch

A Yiddish word for someone who combines wisdom, humor and honor. Say MENSH.

menticide

A way of saying "brainwashing." Menticide means exactly the same thing, but has an even more evil ring to it—as if you're literally killing a mind.

mercurial

Describes someone whose mood changes in a heartbeat. It's also used to describe someone who is always upbeat—the assumption being, perhaps, that they must be depressed in private. In both cases, mercurial people may be difficult, but they are always interesting. Pronounced MEHR-*CURE*-*EE*-*ULL*.

meretricious

Acting flashy in an effort to look like something you're not. A meretricious artist paints with a lot of elaborate brush strokes, but the painting isn't interesting; a meretricious novelist may use fancy language but write a book with no real literary impact. Pronounced MEH-*RIH*-*TRISH*-*USS*.

merman
: The male version of a mermaid. We hear about them less often, but they still make their way into fairy tales. Pronounced like *Superman*, not like Ethel *Merman*.

messianic
: Someone who is messianic acts like a messiah. An excellent way to describe someone who seems to be on a mission from God, or who promotes her ideas with a little too much fervor. Say it MESS-EE-*AN*-IK.

mestizo
: Not a kind of wood used for grilling at a California restaurant, but a person of mixed ancestry, usually part Indian and part African.

metaphrase
: A word-for-word translation, to be distinguished from a *paraphrase*, which summarizes the gist of something. A nice way of saying "verbatim" and sounding high-tech about it.

mete
: To mete out something is to distribute it in measured portions, as in to mete out a punishment to a group of students (for some reason, it seems punishment is always meted). It sounds just like *meat* but spelled differently.

métier | This is another word for forte (see *forte*)—an occupation or activity in which a person has a particularly strong talent. However, unlike forte, which is pronounced *fort*, métier retains its French pronunciation: MET-EE-AY.

metonymy | This is a figure of speech used as a stylistic device by many writers who probably don't know there is a name for it. When you use a metonymy, you substitute an attribute or an example of a thing for the thing itself, evoking one idea by a term that is related. "Today, *the White House* announced a tax hike," for example, or "He gave up *the bottle*." Pronounced MET-*TAHN*-EH-MEE.

mettle | Courageous spirit or vigorous energy. A person of mettle is a brave person who is willing to take action. For some reason, mettle is always being tested.

miasma | The foul-smelling gases given off by decaying matter in marshes and swamps. It's usually used figuratively to describe any confusing subject or event that's hard to sort out. "Her explanation of biogenetics was a miasma of scientific theories and incomprehensible equations." Pronounced MY-AZ-MA.

microeconomics   The opposite of macroeconomics (see *macro-economics*) economics applied to the specific aspects of an economy: supply and demand and the price of sugar, for example.

mien   A person's demeanor, the manner or habits that reflect character or attitude. I can tell by his mien—his furrowed brow, his grimace, the way his hands are clutching his elbows and his foot is tapping—that he's furious. Pronounced MEEN.

milieu   The environment or the conditions surrounding a person or thing; it's kind of like a natural habitat, the place where someone is most comfortable. A dog on a leash set free to run in a park will usually bound about, happy to be in his milieu. Say it MIL-YOO.

millennium   Literally a period of a thousand years, the word can also refer to a supposedly approaching period of general happiness and prosperity, or figuratively to any great length of time: "How have you been? I haven't seen you in a millennium!"

milquetoast

Someone with a character like bread dipped in milk—bland, timid, meek and unassertive. The word refers to the comic-strip character Caspar Milque-toast, created by H. T. Webster. That's why it's spelled with a *qu* and not with a *k*. Say MILK-TOAST.

minatory

Threatening or menacing. When they bark, growl and bare their teeth, dogs are making minatory postures at mail carriers. Pronounced MIN-AT-ORY.

mingy

An onomatopoeic (see *onomatopoeia*) way of saying mean-spirited, stingy and ungenerous. It wraps up the definition nicely in one word, and you're sure that whomever it's directed to will catch the drift, even without knowing the word. It's pronounced MIN-JEE.

minikin

A delicate or diminutive object or person. A porcelain miniature on a shelf is a minikin, but so is a very short and attractive person. Of course, if that person models clothes, you've found a minikin mannequin.

minion

A servile follower of an important or powerful person: a secretary, assistant, associate and the like.

Acolytes (see *acolyte*) and disciples serve voluntarily—minions are caught up in the swirls of the bureaucracy.

minutia

The small, trivial details of something. Someone who worries about minutiae often overlooks the stuff that matters. Pronounced MIN-*NOO*-SHAH.

mirabile dictu

A Latin phrase meaning "wonderful to relate" or "strange to tell." It's the kind of phrase, used sparingly, that can enhance a tale of even the most mundane events: "I went into my daughter's room this morning and—*mirabile dictu*—she had cleaned it up!" It's pronounced MEER-*AB*-EEL-AY *DIK*-TOO.

miscegenation

Marriage or cohabitation of people from different races; the mixture of races by interbreeding. Amazingly enough, this was illegal in Virginia until the mid-1960s. Not to be confused with misogyny (see *misogyny*), which means hatred of women. It's pronounced MISS-*EJJ*-EN-*AY*-SHUN.

miscreant

Depraved or villainously wicked. The word can be used as a noun to describe a person who commits a not-so-serious crime. Fences are posted to keep miscreants out of parks; paints have been developed to discourage miscreants from drawing graffiti on buses and trains. Pronounced MISS-CREE-ANT.

misogamy   Hatred of marriage, a common condition.

misogyny   Hatred of women. You can call a woman-hater a misogynist. Pronounce it MISS-OJ-EN-EE.

misopedia   The last of the *miso-* words we're going to include in this book; it means hatred of children, especially one's own. Certainly a good word to use on a day when the little ones are really getting on your nerves.

mnemonic   A trick used to help remember something, such as remembering someone's birthday because it's the same date as the Battle of Waterloo, or the colors of the spectrum by ROYGBIV, or trigonometry by SOHCAHTOA. Pronounced NEH-MON-IK.

mo   Canadian slang for emotional stress, shortened from *emo*. Usually used with a suffix. A bride who gets a run in her stocking two minutes before the ceremony

145

is moing. A group of students hit with a surprise quiz have a mofest. The word is unique in its ability to capture an all-too-common state of mind. Rhymes with *go*.

modus operandi A Latin phrase that means "mode of operation." Formerly used by Dick Tracy and the Dragnet team to describe the telltale signs a criminal leaves behind, it's now perfect to describe anyone who has a certain way of operating. "Don't worry about Marc—screaming at a meeting is part of his modus operandi." Often shortened to "M.O." Pronounced *MOH-DUS OPP-EHR-AHN-DIE*.

moil Hard work and drudgery, like toil with an *m*. We moiled away for hours over dictionaries to find the best words to include in this book.

mollify To soothe, appease or calm down. Chamberlain tried to mollify Hitler. A father might try to mollify a small child who dropped an ice-cream cone.

monodomous | Living in a single nest, as do bees, ants or humans who can't afford a country house. Pronounced MAH-NOD-AH-MUSS.

monomania | Like an obsession, an overwhelming enthusiasm for a single idea, interest or activity to the exclusion of other pursuits. Great entrepreneurs are often mono-maniacs. They're good for society, but you wouldn't want to marry one.

monotheism | The belief that there is only one God. Atheists are certain that there is no God, while those who are agnostic are unwilling to state an opinion. Distinguish from those who believe that they *are* God. (See also *theomania*.)

mordant | Biting or sarcastic; often combined with wit, as in mordant wit. Someone with a mordant wit is critical with sophisticated humor—Lenny Bruce, for example. (See also *acerbic*.)

morose | Moody, sullen or gloomy. Much more powerful than the overused "depressed." Pronounced MUH-ROHS.

motile

Capable of motion or moving. The word is used most often in microbiological contexts. Plants, animals and people move; cells and bacteria, for example, are motile. If the mold in your refrigerator turns motile, it's time to defrost. Pronounced MOH-*TILL*.

mountebank

This somewhat archaic word means a traveling salesman for quack remedies; it's come to be used to mean any trickster or charlatan. Pronounced MOUNT-*A-BANK*, it's a good word for the stars of those half-hour-long infomercials that sell car wax and nostril-hair removers.

mufti

The civilian clothes donned by one who usually wears a uniform. Sailors might dress in mufti when they leave a ship to visit a port city; a lawyer who comes to work one day in jeans and a t-shirt instead of the usual suit is dressed in mufti. Pronounced MUFF-*TEE*.

mugwump

Someone who acts independently of a political party, or who can't decide, and so remains neutral on political or other issues. The word is also used to mean any mealy-mouthed wimp who refuses to take a stand.

mummer	A person wearing a mask or costume at a parade or a masquerade party. Particularly appropriate to describe participants in the Mardi Gras parade.
munificent	Extremely generous and willing to give. It has a slightly different meaning than *beneficent*, which means willing to do good. Many students receive scholarships thanks to munificent corporate and private sponsors. Pronounced MEW-*NIFF*-EH-SENT.
mussitation	Silently imitating the lip movements of people who are speaking; the kind of behavior that can drive a speaker crazy. (Bet you didn't realize there was a word for this, did you?)
myopia	The medical term for near-sightedness also connotes a more figurative lack of vision, or short-sightedness. People who wear glasses with certain prescriptions suffer from myopia; people who fail to see the consequences of the things they say or do are also *myopic*.
myriad	This adjective simply means "a lot." You can say there were myriad stars in the sky or there were myriad grains of sand on the beach. It's pronounced *MEER*-EE-AD.

N

nabob
: Made famous by Spiro Agnew's description of the press and liberals as "the nattering nabobs of negativism," a nabob is actually a person of great wealth who has made a fortune in a faraway country, especially India. It seems that the Vice President forfeited accurate English in favor of alliteration.

nadir
: A nadir is literally a point in the heavens directly opposite the zenith (see *zenith*). It is often used, however, to connote a low point, as in the nadir of a career or of a life. "He hit the nadir when he lost his house, his job and his wife on one day." Sounds like *Nader*, as in Ralph. (See also *apogee*.)

naissance
: The birth or origin of a concept, an organization, a movement or an idea, as opposed to the *renaissance*,

or rebirth of any of those things. The naissance of rock-and-roll took place in the '50s and '60s; its renaissance was in the '80s. Say NAY-SENSE.

narcolepsy

A condition characterized by an overwhelming desire for brief periods of sleep. The word is often used figuratively to describe feeling terrifically bored: Dull speeches can induce narcolepsy.

nascent

In the formative stages or in the process of being created. (See also *chrysalis*.) The word is best used to describe abstract things such as ideas, feelings or creative works. A nascent feeling would be one that's just beginning to come to consciousness. Pronounced NAY-SENT.

necromancy

A scientific-sounding word for sorcery or witchcraft. Use it when you want something to sound a little more serious than just plain "magic." Say NEK-RUH-MAN-SEE.

nefarious

Very evil or wicked; frequently used to describe cartoon villains. Think of the guy who was always tying Pauline to the railroad tracks. It's also used quite seriously, however: Hitler's henchmen committed nefarious acts. Pronounced NEH-*FARE*-ee-uss.

neophyte

Another way of saying "novice" or "beginner." Someone who takes up tennis for the first time is a neophyte. Pronounced *NEE*-oh-*FIGHT*.

nepenthe

Anything which makes someone forget sorrow, suffering or pain. For some, alcohol is a nepenthe for woes. Others prefer books, movies or shopping. Pronounced NIH-*PEN*-THEE.

nephology

This is the scientific term for the study of clouds. The next time you decide to escape to a field and lie on the grass and find shapes of animals in the clouds, you can say you spent the afternoon studying nephology. Pronounced NEFF-*OL*-OH-JEE.

ne plus ultra

The Latin phrase for the absolute top, the culminating point, the highest degree. For an antique-car collector, finding a Tucker in mint condition would be the *ne plus ultra*. It's pronounced *NAY* PLUSS *OOL*-TRA.

nepotism
: Showing favoritism to friends or relatives in business or politics. If the boss's son is an incompetent idiot and nevertheless is appointed president of the company, chances are that nepotism is at work. Say *NEPP-OH-TIZM*.

nethermost
: A long word for "lowest" or "farthest down," generally used literally—not figuratively. The earth's core is the nethermost region of the planet. The Arctic is the nethermost region of the earth.

nettlesome
: Irritating or annoying. When a car's burglar alarm goes off and blares for hours, that's nettlesome. Particularly in the middle of the night.

niggling
: Excessively petty or nit-picking. A job that involves endless poring over details is niggling work.

nihilism
: Skepticism so complete that it denies there can be any objective basis for truth and, by extension, that there are no morals or values in the universe. A good word for a philosophy that annihilates just about every concept previously thought to exist. Pronounced *NYE-EH-LISM*.

nirvana | This word refers to the Buddhist belief in the release from the cycle of reincarnation that leads to the end of all desire and suffering, but it has come to be used to mean a state akin to heaven on earth. A birthday party with a big cake, lots of candy and ice cream, and piles of presents may be a child's idea of nirvana.

nodus | A complication or a difficulty, kind of like a snag. If you hit a nodus in your research, you're likely to be stuck for days trying to discover the right answer. The plural is nodi. Pronounced *NODE-us*.

noisome | If you think this has to do with an assault on the ears, you've got the wrong organ. Strangely enough, the word means foul-smelling. The diaper bin is noisome. Pronounced *NOY-sum*.

nom de guerre | From the French, it means the same thing as "pseudonym." Robert Zimmerman's *nom de guerre*, for example, is Bob Dylan. If you're going to use it, pronounce it correctly: *NOME DE GAIR*.

nubbin | This word means exactly what it sounds like—a lumpy stub, a bumpy nub. The pills that form on sweaters after you've worn them for a time could just as well be called nubbins.

nubile
Of marriageable age or condition. Since that once meant about 15 years of age, the word came to mean all attractive, young women. Pronounce it *NOO-BILE* or *NOO-BILL*.

nugatory
This is not a reference to a kind of candy. The word means "worthless" or "insignificant." The side effects of a particularly safe medicine, for example, are nugatory. Pronounced *NOOG-AT-OREE*.

nympholepsy
The condition of having deep emotional longings for something unattainable. The best description we've ever heard of first love!

O

obdurate

Cruelly stubborn and hard-hearted; in fact, down-right insensitive. Someone who is hard to convince is stubborn, but someone who won't give in to a simple and reasonable plea is obdurate. Pronounced OB-*DER-IT*.

obfuscate

To confuse. Perfect if you want to confuse someone who's not being clear with you—tell her to stop obfuscating. Say OB-*FUSS-KATE*.

oblique

Like the angle in geometry, which includes lines which are neither parallel nor perpendicular, the word refers to things that are not straight or straight-forward, but indirect. An oblique reference does not directly address the true subject but alludes to it in a secondary or slightly obscure way. It's pronounced OH-*BLEEK*.

obloquy   Public censure or blame, usually verbal. Richard Nixon suffered the obloquy of the press as the events at the Watergate Hotel were revealed. Pronounced OB-*LUH-KWEE*.

obscurantism   Something that is obscure is hard to understand, little known, darkly vague; obscurantism is intentional vagueness or obscurity, a conscious keeping in the dark.

obsequious   An obsequious person fawns, sucks up to or kowtows (see *kowtow*) to someone else. Say OB-*SEE-KWEE-USS*.

obtuse   When describing an idea or explanation, *obtuse* is the opposite of lucid or clear. The CPA's explanation of deferred tax credits was quite obtuse, so the client fired him.

obumbrate   Not to be confused with *adumbrate*, which means to foreshadow, obumbrate means to darken, overshadow or make difficult to see or understand. The word should be used only figuratively. Skies *cloud over* before a rainstorm; weak explanations *obumbrate* the understanding of a scientific concept. Say AH-*BUM-BRATE*.

octogenarian

A person between the ages of 80 and 90, just as a septuagenarian is a person between the ages of 70 and 80. The word has a nice ring to it and sounds a lot better than "senior citizen."

octothorpe

The term created by the Bell System in 1967 for the # or pound sign. Imagine a voice-mail system that instructed callers to "Please press the octothorpe." No one would get any messages!

odalisque

A female slave or concubine in a harem, usually portrayed in 17th- and 18th-century paintings reclining on a divan, swathed in transparent drapery. It's sometimes a good word to use to describe a sexy or sultry (see *sultry*) woman. It's pronounced OH-*DAL-ISK*.

oenology

The science of wine or winemaking. Next time you're offered an expensive wine list and asked to make a choice, you can pass the list to your date and say, "You choose; I'm not an oenologist." If you don't know wines, at least you'll come across as someone with a great vocabulary. Someone who does love wine is an *oenophile*. Pronounced OH-*NAHL*-OH-GEE.

officious — An officious person meddles or interferes without being asked. Overbearing mothers are officious, as are strangers who tell you what you should or shouldn't do. Officials are rarely officious, and officious people are not necessarily officials.

oligarchy — A government in which a small group exercises power over the majority. A company run by a committee is accurately referred to as an oligarchy. Say OH-LIG-ARK-EE.

olio — Yes, it means "oil" in other languages, but the definition we're interested in is what it means in *English*, which is a hodge-podge, a mixture of miscellaneous elements. A grab bag contains an olio of presents; a seafood stew contains an olio of vegetables and fish. (See also *farrago*.)

ombudsman — An official whose job is to investigate complaints made by private citizens about abuses or wrongdoing performed by the government or by the organization he represents. Pronounced OMM-BUDZ-MUHN.

omnifarious Of all varieties or forms; diverse. Nothing to do with being supremely wicked or evil. That's nefarious (see *nefarious*). Say OMM-*NEH*-FAIR-*EE-USS*.

omnificent Having supreme creative power; able to create all things. Many people think God is omnificent; some very egotistical people think they are, too. Say OMM-*NIF*-EH-SENT.

oniomania An irrepressible urge to buy things; the kind of condition that inspires astronomical credit card bills and t-shirt slogans like: "When the going gets tough, the tough go shopping." Pronounced OHN-EE-OH-*MAIN*-EE-A.

onomatopoeia A word that sounds like what it defines (see *flump*). Consider "hiss" or "scratch." Sort of mumble when you say it: AHN-EH-MAHT-EH-PEE-UH.

oppugn Not to be confused with *opine*, which means to offer an opinion, *oppugn* means to fight against or counter-attack. "You always squeeze the toothpaste from the middle!" he said. "You drink from the milk carton and eat crackers in bed!" she oppugned. It's pronounced OH-*PEWN*.

orthography

It's not the study of birds, tooth appliances or support shoes. Orthography is the correct spelling of words according to established rules or usage. Newspaper editors worry about this a lot. Saying "Check the orthography" is much like, "Please proofread this." Say OR-*THOG*-RUH-FREE.

oscitant

An oscitant person acts as if he just took a Valium or is badly in need of a nap: lazy, drowsy, inattentive and unfocused. It can be used to describe a physical condition or a state of mind. More temporary than narcolepsy (see *narcolepsy*). Say OSS-IH-TENT.

osculate

To kiss and/or hug. Like pulchritude (see *pulchritude*), this is an ugly word for a wonderful action. The word was probably created by a lexicographer who didn't do enough osculating.

ossify

To turn to bone. This word can be used both literally and figuratively. It means to become brittle and bone-hard (like a slice of bread after it's been lying in the sun for a few days) or to become mentally brittle or rigid in attitude and outlook.

otiose

Idle, useless and unnecessary. Not to be confused with *adipose*, which means fat. When companies make cutbacks, they can fire the otiose personnel and they won't be sued for discriminating against overweight people. Say *OH-TEE-OSE*.

oubliette

A hidden dungeon that can only be entered from above; the kind of word that pops up frequently in fairy tales that feature monsters. Fair maidens and princesses are always being thrown into oubliettes by evil monsters. It's pronounced *OO-BLEE-ET*.

ovine

If a cow is a bovine (see *bovine*), what's a sheep? Ovine! Use this word to describe sheep-like behavior. This could include lack of individual initiative, a tendency to say *baaah*, or wool growing on one's back.

oxhaft

Approximately 57 gallons. Useful in hyperbolic (see *hyperbole*) statements such as, "I'd like an oxhaft of double decaf espresso please."

oxymoron

This word describes a phrase that is internally contradictory. We like "jumbo shrimp" and "deposed President-for-Life."

P

padnag

Literally, it means an old, slow horse, like a nag, but it's a good word for describing an old piece of well-loved but slow office equipment, or a broken-down car that still gets around. It's pronounced *PAD-NAG*.

paillette

A large sequin or spangle, the kind sewn onto evening gowns to make them glitter. Now you know what those sparkly things are called! Pronounced *PAL-YET*.

paladin

A brave knight or a chivalrous champion; a good word to use for that person you've been hoping will ride in on a white horse and save the day. When that savior rides in, call him or her a *PAL-AH-DIN*.

palaver

Idle chitchat or meaningless chatter. Adults make palaver at cocktail parties, as do teenagers on the telephone. It's pronounced *PELL-AV-ER*.

palimpsest

A piece of parchment or other tablet, used for early writing, that was erased and reused a second time. This is the kind of word that crops up in auctions for famous manuscripts and at antique stores that deal in old books and prints. It is most often used figuratively, however, to connote a piece of work in which a previously completed and erased work shines through. An example—math homework in which a teacher can see the ways that a student attempted to solve a problem before coming up with the final answer. Say *PAL-IMP-SEST*.

palindrome

A word or phrase that reads the same backward as forward, such as "Madam, I'm Adam" or "RADAR" or "A man, a plan, a canal—Panama!"

palliative

Something that eases or soothes a situation, feeling or condition without solving or curing it. Aspirin, for example, is a palliative because it can take away the fever caused by a virus, but can't cure the virus itself. Giving a crying child a lollipop after an allergy shot has a palliative effect. Say *PAL-EE-AH-TIV*.

panacea

A cure for all ills. Since nothing is a cure-all, the word is usually used in the negative, as in: "The new government policy is not a panacea for all of society's ills, but it will relieve certain economic burdens of the poor." Pronounced PAN-A-*SEE*-AH.

pandemic
Distributed or prevalent practically throughout the world; universal. Homelessness is a problem pandemic to every urban society. Throughout the world, *Coca-Cola* is the pandemic drink of choice. A pandemic is similar to an epidemic, but a pandemic is much more widespread.

panegyric
A speech that lavishly praises someone or something. A homeopathic (see *homeopathy*) doctor might deliver a panegyric on the healing qualities of ginseng. It's pronounced PAN-IH-*JYE*-RIK or PAN-IH-*JEER*-IK.

panjandrum
A pompous, self-important official, such as the people who check your bags at customs or the oh-so-helpful assistants behind the desks in motor vehicle bureaus. If you're really frustrated by the way they treat you, you could probably call them panjandrums and get away with it. Say PAN-*JAN*-DREM.

panoply

A complete array of something that is usually quite splendid in its breadth and size. "A panoply of flowers blanketed the open field." "A panoply of desserts covered the wedding buffet table." Say *PAN-EH-PLEE*.

papilote

Bet you didn't know there was a word for this. It's the little piece of colorful fringed paper wrapped around the end of a lamb chop. You see fewer and fewer of them, but they're still around in certain fine restaurants. Pronounce it *PAP-ILL-OAT*.

paraclete

A person you call upon to intercede. Referees, umpires, and judges are all paracletes. Pronounced *PAR-AH-CLEET*.

paradigm

A model example; the standard to hold up for comparison. Politicians hold up the decline of the U.S. auto industry as a paradigm for Japanese strategy in other areas. Pronounced *PAR-A-DIME*.

paralogize

This odd verb means "to draw illogical conclusions from a series of facts." An example: after being told about a pet that barks, likes bones, chases cats and wags its tail, you say, "Oh, I didn't know you had a parrot." It's pronounced *PAR-AHL-OH-JIZE*.

paraph

The word for the elaborate flourishes people add to their signatures to make them unique. Think John Hancock. In this age of Bic pens, they're rapidly disappearing. Pronounced PAR-*EFF* or PAR-*EFF*. (See also *idiograph*.)

paravalent

Sexually potent only in unusual circumstances—a fancy word for kinky.

parlous

You might think this has something to do with speech or parlance, but it doesn't. It means perilous, dangerous and difficult to escape from. "After a number of parlous incidents in the jungle, which included being bitten by snakes and shot at by poachers, the tourists decided to take their next vacation in Miami." It's pronounced PAR-*LUSS*.

parochial

Excessively narrow in outlook; having backward views stemming from a lack of worldly experience. People who live in small towns are often considered parochial in their attitudes and beliefs. Don't confuse with parochial schools, which, while often parochial, may not be. It's pronounced PAR-*OKE-EE-AL*.

paroxysm

A fit or outburst, often of emotion, as in: "The comedian inspired the crowd to paroxysms of laughter." Pronounced PAHR-OX-IZM.

parure

A matched set of jewelry, such as earrings and a necklace; the kind of word seen most often on museum cards and in auction catalogues. Save the word for when you're talking about diamonds and emeralds—not Bakelite. Pronounced PUH-ROOR.

parvenu

A subtler word for what we usually call *nouveau riche*. A parvenu is someone who has recently acquired money or social status, but has not yet acquired the appropriate style or manner. The word can also be used to describe any newcomer to a situation who has not yet learned to handle his role or responsibility, such as a young worker who gets a big promotion and acts obnoxious and superior around the people who were his closest colleagues the day before. Pronounced PAR-VEN-YOO. (See also *arriviste*.)

passementerie

The squiggly, braided trimming you see on clothing such as matador's suits, felt sombreros or other clothing. (How did you live without knowing that?) It's pronounced PASS-A-MENT-AIR-EE.

pastiche
: A literary or musical work composed of a mixture of borrowed themes or styles. Some might say that rap is a pastiche of soul music, poetry and reggae. Pronounced *PAHSS-TEESH*.

pathetic fallacy
: The attribution of human emotions to elements of nature; for example, describing a rainy day as a sad or depressing day. Distinguish from anthropomorphism (see *anthropomorphism*), which attributes human characteristics to inanimate objects.

pathos
: Any work or situation that inspires pity or sorrow. It should be distinguished from bathos (see *bathos*), which chronicles a fall from the sublime to the commonplace. Pronounced *PAYTH-OSE* or *PAY-THOSS*.

patina
: The outermost layer of a metal surface, most particularly the filmy green layer that forms on bronze or copper after oxidation that is thought to add beauty. You could be figurative and use it to describe a person's manner and appearance. It's pronounced *PAT-IH-NUH*. Also *patine*, pronounced *PAH-TEEN*.

patois
Local dialect or jargon; a language peculiar to people of a certain area that is distinct from the standard language. Natives of Caribbean islands, for instance, converse in French or English or Dutch with tourists, but speak patois among themselves. It's pronounced *PAT-WAH*.

patronize
Two very different but useful meanings. To patronize a store means to do business there, while to patronize a fellow human is to condescend to him or her: "*Of course*, I'll be there on time. Let me give you a signed statement."

peccadillo
The word refers to small sins or minor offenses, often sexual. When a married woman has a brief affair, she has a peccadillo. If a worker borrows a few dollars from petty cash and takes a long time to pay it back, that's also a peccadillo.

peccant
This does not mean spicy and flavorful; that's piquant (see *piquant*). Guilty of a moral sin. Perhaps the woman who had a *peccadillo* (see above) could be considered peccant. Pronounced *PECK-ANT*.

pedagogue This word can simply mean "teacher," but more often it has the same meaning as *pedant* (see below), an extremely opinionated teacher who tries to force those opinions on others, ignoring common sense in favor of theoretical knowledge.

pedant A teacher, but the implication is one who is tiresome, and always focused on small details. "Be careful with your new-found vocabulary skills, or you'll become a pedant and no one will talk to you any more." (See *pedagogue* above.)

pellucid Transparent or translucent; as long as you can see through something, you may call it pellucid. Say PEL-*LOO*-SID.

penicil No, it's not a writing implement. In fact, it's the kind of short, bristly tufts of hair or fur you find along the backs of caterpillars. A great word for crossword puzzles or for teasing a friend who just got a punk haircut. Say PEN-*I*-SILL.

penultimate Second to last, whether it's your place on line, or the next-to-the-last paragraph. The letter *t* is the

penultimate letter in the word *penultimate*. Say PEN-
UL-TIM-IT.

perdition

Utter ruin of the spirit; eternal damnation. Even if
you don't believe in Hell, you can believe in perdition; it has no necessary religious connotation, but
suggests ultimate punishment for moral sin. Say PER-
DISH-IN.

peregrinate

A verb that means to wander or travel with no plans
or itinerary. Jack Kerouac wrote of his peregrinations
in *On the Road*. It's pronounced PER-EG-RIN-ATE.
(See also *peripatetic*.)

peremptory

Dictatorial or authoritarian; allowing no room for
argument. Brusque. "Go to your room!" is a peremptory order.

perfervid

Extremely ardent or intense; fervent to the nth
degree. Zealots are perfervid, whatever their cause.
Say PER-FUR-VID. (See also *messianic*.)

perfidious

Treacherous; nefarious; wicked. There are lots of
words for evil; perfidious carries a note of disloyalty or

betrayal. Benedict Arnold was perfidious. To call him a perfidious traitor would be redundant.

perfunctory Routine; performed automatically, without thought or feeling. A job done perfunctorily reveals no particular passion and seems careless. A perfunctory greeting lacks enthusiasm. Say *PER-FUNK-TOR-EE*.

peripatetic An adjective or noun that means traveling from place to place; itinerant. Migrant workers are peripatetic. You can also be peripatetic by reading this book in no particular order. (See also *peregrinate*.)

perorate This word is a mouthful, as is its meaning, which is: to make a lengthy speech, often summarizing everything that's been said before. When you try, say *PER-UH-RATE*.

perquisite Abbreviated to "perk." The perquisites of a job are the advantages or fees that come in addition to the regular salary, such as use of a company car or paid vacation time; fringe benefits.

persevere To persist. Never give up. Not spelled perservere, a common error. Say *PURR-SIH-VEER*.

persiflage   Light banter. (See also *bavardage*.) Pronounced *PER-SIF-LAJ*.

pertinacious   Holding firmly to a belief or opinion; unwilling to be drawn away from a previously held idea. (See also *obdurate*.) Pronounced *PERT-IN-AY-SHUSS*.

peruse   To review thoroughly, study carefully. Often misused to mean "skim." Say *PURR-OOZE*.

pestle   As in "mortar and pestle," the traditional tools used by a pharmacist. The pestle is the stick that looks like a knee bone; the mortar is the little bowl that holds the stuff to be crushed.

pettifogger   A person overly concerned with details, such as certain accountants or lawyers for the opposing side. A pettifogger is someone who nit-picks, a niggler (see *niggler*).

pharisee   A sanctimonious, self-righteous hypocrite; someone who loudly criticizes others for behavior he engages in himself. Say *FAIR-IS-HE*, even though he's not fair at all.

phatic — This word is used to describe language that conveys friendship or sociability rather than information. Greetings exchanged among friends at a party, or conversations on a receiving line at a wedding or funeral, are generally phatic. It's pronounced *FAT-IK*.

phenology — Not to be confused with *phrenology*; that's the study of the skull as an indicator of mental characteristics. *Phenology* is the study of the role of climate in annually recurring natural phenomena, such as bird migration, animal hibernation, plant flowerings and so forth.

philipic — Sounds like a cure for indigestion, but it's more likely to cause a stomachache than cure one. A philipic is a hostile speech that denounces a person or thing with great bitterness. Demonstrators deliver philipics during rallies; furious spouses deliver philipics against erring partners. Pronounced *PHIL-IPP-ICK*.

philistine — An uncultured person; someone who has no interest or knowledge of art or civilization. Someone who'd rather go skateboarding than to a museum would be considered funloving by some and a philistine by others. If you don't want to sound like a philistine, pronounce it *FILL-ISS-TEEN*.

philobat

A lover of travel. Someone who takes taxis every day is not a philobat; someone who's been around the world several times is either a philobat or has a very tough job in sales. It's pronounced *FIL-OH-BAT*.

picaresque

Roguish or devilish. Don Quixote was the original picaresque character (see *quixotic*). Take care to distinguish from *picturesque*, which describes pleasant scenery. Pronounced *PICK-AH-REHSK*.

piebald

Often used to describe horses, cows or cats. It means covered with irregular patches of different colors, especially black and white. Think of the cows on Ben and Jerry's ice-cream containers.

pilaster

A fancy word for a fake column, the kind that doesn't stand freely, but runs along the walls of rooms that are trying to resemble the Colosseum in Rome or an ancient Greek ruin. Pronounce *PIE-LASS-TER*.

pindling	Frail or puny. Distinguished in usage from *piddling*, which means trivial or trifling.
pintle	Like peanut butter is to jelly, a pintle is inextricably linked with a *gudgeon*, a metal pivot. The pintle is a little pin that sticks into the hinge-like holes of the gudgeon, holding a rudder to the back of a small sailboat. When you're searching for a figurative phrase to describe an interlocked set, say, "They fit like a pintle and gudgeon."
piquant	Not to be confused with peccant (see *peccant*). A pleasantly sharp or spicy flavor. Good marinara sauce, Cajun ribs, Szechwan beef and chicken Vindaloo are all piquant. Classier than saying "hot," and having to explain you mean spicy. Pronounced (once your mouth cools down) *PEEK-ANT OR PEEK-UNT*.
pismire	Another word for "ant." You can use it to refer to the little bug, or to describe something equally tiny. It's a good word to use when you're annoyed with someone, as in: "I'm tired of your pismire hobbies that leave no time for more important things." Pronounced *PISS-MIRE*.

plangent

Deep, low and resonantly mournful. Used to describe the music at a funeral or the mooing of a lone cow in an open field. Pronounced *PLAN-JENT*.

pledget

A small wad of cotton or paper used to absorb liquid, such as the little patch of tissue you use to staunch the blood when you cut yourself shaving.

Pleistocene era

Of all the geological periods, probably the most interesting to remember since it includes the Ice Ages and the evolution of early man. It is also the geological epoch that immediately precedes our present epoch. If you haven't seen someone for a while, you can hyperbolize (see *hyperbole*) back to the Pleistocene era. It's pronounced *PLY-STESS-SEEN*.

plenipotentiary

A person vested with the full power to act on behalf of someone else. It's more than a power of attorney. A parent may act as a plenipotentiary for a child; an ambassador may be sent to act as a plenipotentiary for the ruler of a country. Pronounce *PLEHN-EH-PEH-TEN-SHEE-EHR-EE*.

plethora	An excess; more than enough to choose from; a glut. Imelda Marcos, for example, had a plethora of shoes in her closet. Say *PLETH-OR-AH*.
plunder	To pillage. "Plunder and pillage" is redundant. Pick one and use it exclusively.
plutocracy	Government by the wealthy—not by the dog from the Walt Disney cartoons. Say *PLOO-TOCK-REH-SEE*.
pococurante	How's this for a great insult? Someone who is careless or shows little concern or interest for a job or responsibility. A person who consistently leaves work early and takes too many days off is a pococurante; so is a student who doesn't attend classes or hand in assignments. Pronounced *PO-CO-CYOOR-ANT-EE*.
poi	Mashed taro root. Rhymes with *boy*. A very mushy, traditional Hawaiian dish that hasn't attracted much attention on the mainland.
polemic	A controversy or an argument made to refute something (similar in tone to a diatribe; see *diatribe*). *Das Kapital* was a polemic against the injustices of capitalism. It's pronounced *PUH-LEM-IK*.

politesse
Like politeness, it means refined or courteous behavior. It's just a more refined and polite way of saying so. With great politesse, the butler bowed and led the guests into the drawing room. In general, people with drawing rooms act with politesse. It's pronounced POLE-EE-*TESS*.

poltroon
Sounds like an army expression, but it's not. Unless, of course, you're AWOL—the word means "coward."

polyandry
You know *monogamy* and *bigamy*, but this word belongs exclusively to women. It's the act of having more than one husband at a time. Don't confuse it with *polygyny* (that's having more than one wife at a time) or *polygamy* (either spouse having more than one partner at a time).

polyglot
A polyglot is able to speak several languages fluently. A polyglot group is composed of people who speak a variety of languages, such as the U.N.'s General Assembly.

polymath
This is neither a higher form of mathematics nor someone who's taken a lot of algebra courses. A

polymath is someone who knows a great deal about a lot of different subjects; a well-educated, intelligent person with eclectic interests.

polymorphous
: Occurring in any number of varied forms, such as the voice of a mockingbird which can imitate other birds or the changing colors of a chameleon. Say POL-EE-MORF-US.

polysemous
: Ambiguous in the sense of having several different meanings. An artfully concise book title that could be interpreted in several different ways is polysemous. Abraham Lincoln's famous book review, "People who like this sort of thing will find this the sort of thing they like" is polysemous. Pronounce it POLL-EE-SEEM-US.

pontificate
: To express opinions in a pompous, overly ponderous way. (See also *pedant*.)

popinjay
: A vain, narcissistic, empty-headed person of either sex—the kind of person you date once and never again.

popple — Just like it sounds, it means to tumble about or bob up and down irregularly. Boiling water popples in the pot; clothes popple past the circular window of a dryer when they're drying; buoys popple on the surface of a lake on a windy day.

portico — A portico is an open porch consisting of four columns and a roof (but no walls) that you often see along the sides of old colonial houses. These days, people tend to enclose them and use them as sun porches.

portmanteau — A blend or combination of uses. The word is most often used as a noun to describe words that combine or blend other words like "smog" or "docudrama." It's pronounced PORT-MAN-*TOH*.

postiche — Not to be confused with a pastiche (see *pastiche*). A postiche is a superfluous ornament, usually added to a sculpture or work that is already finished. Think of adding earrings to the Statue of Liberty or a mustache to the Mona Lisa. Pronounced POST-*EESH*.

postpositive

A word that is always used after another. For example, manqué (see *manqué*) never stands alone, instead we say "artist manqué."

postprandial

Something that happens after dinner, such as a postprandial walk or postprandial snifter of brandy. If it happens before dinner, it's called *preprandial*— imagine a cocktail or, if it's a weekend, a nap.

pother

It's kind of like "bother" when it's used as a noun. A pother is a fuss or commotion: "Don't make such a pother about it. We promised we'd visit our relatives, and we're going."

preciosity

An excessive fastidiousness, particularly in the use of language. It refers to something precious or affected, not precious in the ordinary sense of the word. It's pronounced PRESH-EE-OSS-IH-TEE.

précis

A summary. Book reviews frequently contain a précis of the plot of the book discussed. Pronounced PRAY-SEE.

predicable   Something that can be stated as true or that can be proved. Pronounced *PRED-IK-AH-BULL*.

predormition   The period of semiconsciousness before sleep, when you either begin to dream or to worry (in which case you may not sleep at all).

prepossess   Has nothing to do with a pawn shop. To impress favorably either beforehand or immediately. Someone who makes a good first impression is very prepossessing.

presage   It means to forewarn or to portend. The first snowflake presages winter. You may know the word, but do you know that it's pronounced *PRESS-IJ*?

preterhuman   This is another way of saying superhuman or beyond the powers of mere mortals. (Clark Kent must have thought that "Preterman" sounded pretty silly.) It's pronounced *PREE-TER-HYOO-MAN*.

preternatural   Beyond the course of nature—almost supernatural. The forest can be preternaturally quiet—so quiet that it's not natural. Pronounced *PREE-TER-NATCH-OOR-UL*.

prevaricate — Not quite fibbing, but close. When you prevaricate, you make vague or misleading statements without telling an outright falsehood. If you don't want to go somewhere and you're feeling healthy, "I can't make it tonight. I'm sick" is a lie; "I'm not sure I can make it tonight. I'll get there if I can but don't wait for me" is a prevarication. Say *PRIH-VARE-IH-KATE*.

prima facie — A Latin term for self-evident or apparent. Getting caught with your hand in the cookie jar is prima facie evidence of theft. It's pronounced *PREE-MA FASH-EE*.

primer — A book that covers the basics of a subject. Originally used to describe the books used in one-room school-houses, it can now be applied to software documentation or basic texts in any subject. Careful with the pronunciation. Rhymes with *simmer*.

primogenitor — Often confused to mean first-born or heir apparent. In fact, it means ancestor. Pronounced *PRIME-OH-JEN-IT-OR*.

pristine — When something is pristine, it retains its original or pure form. Most commonly, works of art or antiques in perfect condition are described as pristine. A photograph that has no creases, tears or stains is pristine. Say *PRISS-TEEN*.

proactive
Often misused to mean "active." It means the opposite of reactive. Action that is proactive precedes, even promotes or prevents, a situation. Politicians are reactive; good chess players are proactive.

probity
Honesty; integrity; incorruptibility. Has nothing to do with probability or wills. Pronounced *PROH-BIT-EE*.

prognosticate
To predict from available facts, to foresee or prophesize. The word has to do with making a judgment based on available information rather than using spiritual or astrological signs. Economists prognosticate the future state of the economy based on certain indicators; pollsters prognosticate the outcome of elections based on polling results.

prolicide
The killing of one's own or other children. The kind of act you'd like to commit when the four-year-old that's sitting right in front of you on a trans-Atlantic flight begins to scream. Pronounce it *PRO-LISS-IDE*.

prolix — Unnecessarily wordy; verbose. 'Nuff said. Pronounced *PROH-LIX*.

Promethean — Daringly original; innovative and creative. In Greek mythology, Prometheus got in big trouble for stealing fire from Mount Olympus and giving it to mankind. Say *PRO-MEE-THEE-AN*.

propinquity — Closeness or nearness, either physically (as in proximity) or spiritually (as in affinity). Something lying right next to something else is in propinquity to it; two people who share spiritual, philosophical or intellectual ideas also have a propinquity.

prosaic — It doesn't mean fancy—exactly the opposite. The word literally means commonplace or ordinary but has an added touch of meaning boring and dull. Apricot tea is exotic; orange pekoe is prosaic. Pronounced *PRO-ZAY-IK*.

proscribe — The noun for this verb is *proscription* and it means almost the exact opposite of "prescription." To proscribe something is to forbid it or label it dangerous. Tea and toast would be prescribed for an upset stomach; red-hot chili peppers would be proscribed. Say *PROH-SCRIBE*.

proselytize

Someone who proselytizes tries to convert others by using strongly persuasive language or convincing argument. It implies a certain degree of oppressive lecturing. Demonstrators proselytize about their causes, as do zealots, fanatics and members of some organized religions. Pronouncing it is easy—*PROSS-ELL-IT-IZE*. Just try to remember how to spell it!

protean

Easily changeable from one form to another. Someone who can fit into any social situation, changing types to fit the circumstances, is protean. Pronounced *PROH-TEE-AN*.

Proustian

This is a reference to Marcel Proust's novel *Remembrance of Things Past*, in which the protagonist takes a bite of a pastry he enjoyed as a child, and the taste of the pastry evokes a flood of childhood memories. The term has come to mean any sensory experience that provokes a flood of nostalgia. When an adult has a glass of chocolate milk and an Oreo, he or she is likely to have a Proustian experience. The smell of newly-mown grass is often Proustian, evoking memories of summer camp or trips to the country. Say *PROOST-EE-AN*.

provenance

Place of origin or source. Frequently used when obtaining information about a work of art or an antique. The next time you're in a posh antique store and want to give the impression that you belong there, say to the owner, "Can you tell something about the provenance of this crystal thingee?" Say *PRAHV-EN-ENCE*.

puce

No one is quite clear about what color puce really is. Some say chartreuse; others guess pinkish-purple. Others shrug and offer, "Green?" Well, here's the official answer: the word comes from the French word for "flea" and designates the color of a flea, which, if you put that flea under a microscope, you would discover is purplish-brown. Rhymes with *loose*.

puerile

There is great debate about the pronunciation of this word, which means "childish or immature." Grown-ups who go around their offices sticking "Kick Me" signs on the backs of their coworkers are considered puerile, especially by the people who get the signs stuck on their backs. The preferred pronunciation is not *PWER-IL*, but *PYOOR-IL*.

pulchritude

The opposite of what it sounds like. Someone of great pulchritude is absolutely beautiful. The only known use of this word is to confuse those who hear it. Pronounced *PULK-RI-TOOD*.

punctilious

Not someone who knows where to put punctuation—although it could be. A punctilious person is someone who is meticulous and pays attention to details, punctuation or otherwise.

purlieu

There are several definitions for this word, but the most usable one is a habitat or a place one frequents. The local bar is the purlieu for certain folks; the library is the purlieu for others. When you are in your particular purlieu, it becomes your milieu (see *milieu*). Say it *PURR-LYOO*.

pursy

Short of breath, especially because of being too fat. The obese man in front of you who is slowly climbing the steps and panting heavily is pursy. Vivid word, isn't it?

putsch | The German word for a sudden uprising and take-over. It generally refers to a government coup, but if a group of coworkers get together to kick out their superior and take over her responsibilities, that's a putsch too. Rhymes with *butch*.

Q

quagmire

This word means swamp or bog or any earth that shakes when trodden upon, but it is probably more often used figuratively to mean a murky mess. A teenager's room might be a quagmire of dirty clothes, food wrappers and old magazines; a bad answer to an essay question on an exam might be a quagmire of poorly expressed thoughts and conflicting ideas. Say KWAG-MY-ER.

quash

This is not a vegetable akin to eggplant or zucchini; it's a verb that means "to put an end to" or "to get rid of." Mostly you quash ideas or feelings, not people (that's *murder*).

quay

An often misused word. A quay is a wharf, not a bay. So a walk out on Hawk's Quay in Florida won't get you wet. And it is pronounced KEY, not KWAY.

quasi

A word you always see in combination with another word, as in "*quasi*-intelligence," "*quasi*-healthy," "*quasi*-important." It means seeming to be, but not really being. A quasi-intelligent person probably sounds smart and insightful, but if you listen carefully he may be saying very little. Quasi-healthy food may be labeled "all natural" but contain lots of sugar or fat. Pronounced *QWAY-ZEE* or *KWAH-ZEE*.

querulous

Complaining in a whining, peevish sort of way. Parents become irritated or annoyed when their children misbehave; children become querulous when they're forced to behave. A querulous adult is probably acting like a child. It's pronounced *KWER-YOU-LUSS*.

quidnunc

A gossip. The only word that ends in *unc*.

quid pro quo

Tit for tat; something given in return. If you are a vengeful person and I'm nasty to you, quid pro quo you'll be nasty to me. Pronounced *KWID PRO KWO*.

quiescent

A nice word for "motionless" or "still." If someone isn't talking, he's quiet; if he's lying down, he's sleeping or relaxing; if he's sitting motionless on a couch and staring into space, he's quiescent (or catatonic). A still lake at dawn is quiescent. The coolest use of this word is for the Popsicle, which is quiescently frozen. It's pronounced *KWEE-ESS-ENT*.

quincunx
A hard word to say (and even harder to spell). It means the arrangement of five objects with one at each corner of a square, and the remaining one in the center. Think of the arrangement of a five of hearts on a playing card (or anything else arranged like the five on a playing card). Pronounced *KWING-KUNKS*.

quisling
A collaborating spy. The word derives from Major Vidkun Quisling, who aided the German invaders of his native Norway during World War II. It can be used to refer to anyone who spies on his own group for the benefit of a competitor.

quixotic
This word is often misused to mean "flaky" or "changeable." In fact, as anyone who remembers the story of Don Quixote knows, a quixotic person is someone who is romantic and idealistic and pursues lofty but impractical goals. One grows impatient with

quixotic people but rarely dislikes them. It's pronounced *KWIKS-OTT-ICK*.

quotidian   Ordinary, common, or occurring every day, such as a dose of vitamins. Pronounced *KWOH-TIDD-EE-IN*.

R

raconteur
A great storyteller; the kind of person who tells wonderfully amusing anecdotes with split-second timing and a great choice of words. Mark Twain is perhaps the most famous example. Say RACK-ON-TOUR.

raffish
Tacky, cheap or in bad taste. The word can refer to people or things. A tourist dressed in a Hawaiian shirt and plaid shorts looks raffish, as do most of the doo-dads sold in airport souvenir shops.

raillery
Not the stuff trains run on. Pronounced RAY-LER-EE, it's another word for good-natured banter and light teasing. (See also *bavardage*.)

ramekin
This belongs with papilote (see *papilote*) in the "Obscure Restaurant" list. A ramekin is the lidless

ceramic baking dish used for individual servings of foods such as French onion soup. Say *RAM-EH-KIN*.

randy

Lustful or lecherous. In the '50s, this word was used instead of "horny."

rankle

To cause long-lasting anger or resentment. Nasty, superior and unfair employers rankle their employees.

rapacious

Plundering or taking by force. Rapacious soldiers don't just occupy a town, they pillage it. (See also *plunder*.)

rara avis

A Latin phrase for an unusual person or thing—a rare bird. A very scholarly way of saying one-in-a-million. Pronounce it *RAIR-UH AY-VISS*.

rasher

One thin slice of bacon is a rasher, although many people now use the word to mean an order of several slices. Next time you order breakfast, ask for six or seven rashers of bacon.

ratiocinate

To reason by use of formal logic. That would include inducing, deducing, and every method in between.

When you give a great deal of thought to a problem, you can say you figured it out by ratiocination. Pronounced *RASH-EE-OH-SIN-ATE*.

recalcitrant | Rebellious, stubborn and disobedient. The word is generally reserved to describe difficult children (or adults who act like difficult children). "I begged him to come to the concert, but he was recalcitrant, refusing to go because no Motown music was going to be played at the Philharmonic."

recidivate | To relapse. Most often used to describe convicts who are released from prison, then commit more crimes. Chain smokers who try to quit are prone to recidivism. Pronounced *REE-SID-I-VATE*.

recondite | Esoteric; little known; obscure. References to medieval history texts, the mating rituals of rare Australian birds, or Norwegian jazz, for example, are recondite. Pronounced *RECK-EHN-DITE*.

reconnoiter | To engage in a preliminary survey of something in order to gain information. This word was first a military term but has expanded to mean checking

anything out in advance of doing it. You can recon-
noiter a parking lot for available spaces, for instance,
before driving your car in. It's pronounced REE-CON-
OY-TER and can also be spelled reconnoitre (but that
would be affected—see *preciosity*).

recreant

This has nothing to do with play or outdoor sports;
a recreant is a traitor or a coward, someone who
abandons his friends, family or country. It's pronounced REK-REE-ANT.

rectitude

Moral righteousness or integrity. People who say or
do things with rectitude have generally been truly
good. There's no self-righteousness or hypocrisy
involved. Mother Theresa has rectitude, as do a lot
of good people who are less famous.

red herring

Something introduced merely to divert attention
from a more important and possibly controversial
issue. Appears in Agatha Christie mysteries all the
time. In a different context, it's also used to denote a
printed prospectus detailing the terms of issuance of
shares of a new corporation.

redolent

A very musical word for fragrant or sweet-smelling. Gardens are redolent in spring, as are the newly washed heads of infants. Pronounced *RED-A-LENT*.

refractory

Hard to manage; resistant to conventional treatment. A child who refuses to obey is refractory. So is a malignant tumor that does not respond to chemotherapy or any other conventional cancer therapy.

refulgent

Shining or gleaming, like harbor lights or stars on a clear night. *RIH-FUHL-JENT* is the way to say it.

reify

To make an abstract concept concrete. A written contract, for example, may reify the terms of an agreement that have been discussed in a meeting. It's pronounced *REE-IFF-EYE*.

rejoinder

A response to an answer, usually a good response but not quite as clever as a riposte (see *riposte*).

remonstrate

To plea in protest; kind of like a verbal version of "to demonstrate." Striking workers may demonstrate in picket lines and then arrange meetings to remonstrate with the management. Pronounced *REH-MAHN-STRATE*.

remontado

A person who escapes the pressures of civilization by fleeing to the mountains (or the islands, or...). Say REE-MAHN-*TAH*-DOH.

renege

You probably know what it means to go back on one's word or break a promise. But did you know it had an *e* on the end? It's pronounced REE-*NEGG*.

reprobate

A depraved or unprincipled person; someone who is all but morally hopeless. It's pronounced *REP*-ROH-BATE.

restive

The opposite of restful, this word means fidgety, nervously impatient and uneasy. A variation on *restless*.

retrench

To reduce or cut back. During a recession, people tend to retrench, spending less on luxury items and entertainment.

rimple

Not a hat worn by a nun or a medieval lady; that's a wimple. Rimple is just another word for a wrinkle or crease. Aging persons have rimples around their eyes; poorly packed clothes come out of the suitcase filled with rimples.

riposte — A sharp, usually clever, retort; the exact opposite of an esprit d'escalier (see *esprit d'escalier*). Originally a fencing term. It's pronounced REE-*POST*.

rodomontade — A bragging, boastful speech. None of us could bear to listen to another word of that arrogant pedant's rodomontade. (See also *pedant*.) It's pronounced *ROD*-EM-ON-*TAID*.

roman à clef — Literally, "novel with a key." A novel in which the characters are real people disguised by fictitious names. Pronounced ROH-*MAN* AH *CLAY*.

roué — A rake; a dissipated, lascivious man, but with a touch of the dashing romantic. Don Juan took the cake. It's pronounced ROO-*AY*.

rubric — Not the multicolored puzzle cube, but close. A set of regulations for behavior or procedure. Say *ROOB*-RIC.

rumbelow — A combination of meaningless syllables that evoke a feeling or mood, such as "yo-ho-ho" or "tra-la-la" or "lah-di-dah." Pronounced *RUM*-BEH-LOH.

ruthful

The opposite of ruthless is indeed a word; it means having pity, compassion or remorse. To use it as a noun, just say "ruth": "At the funeral, the murderer showed ruth."

S

sage
We know it's a spice, but it also means "extremely wise." In particular, it refers to the kind of wisdom that comes from experience rather than from books.

salacious
Yet another word for lustful and lecherous. (See also *licentious*, *randy* and *lascivious*.) Pronounced SAHL-*AY*-SHUSS.

salient
The most notable; the things that stand out as the most important. The salient features of a product are the things that make it worth buying. It's pronounced *SAIL*-YENT.

salmagundi
A mixture or miscellaneous collection. (See also *farrago* and *olio*.)

salubrious
Promoting good health. Spa water, vitamins and oat bran (and a slew of other items that are health-food store staples) are said to be salubrious. Say it SAL-OO-BREE-USS.

sang froid
Composure or calm in the face of danger, difficulty or annoyance. The guards in front of Buckingham Palace maintain their sang froid under all circumstances. Pronounced SANG FRWAH.

sanguine
Cheerful and optimistic. After looking through the annual report, he felt sanguine about his investment. It's pronounced SANG-WIN.

sans souci
Resorts are fond of naming themselves with this French phrase, perhaps because it means "carefree." Peggy Lee sings a great song about it. She pronounces it SAHN SUE-SEE.

saporific
Not to be confused with soporific (see *soporific*), saporific with an *a* means "giving flavor." Dull lectures, B-movies, and tranquilizers are soporifics; red pepper, hot fudge, and curry are all saporifics.

sardonic   Bitter or scornful. It can describe a sense of humor, a personality type or a work of art.

sartorial   Relating to clothing, especially men's clothing. The emperor who wanted new clothes called on the sartorial skills of everyone in his kingdom.

saturnalia   A period of wild revelry. Bacchanals (see *bacchanal*) are drunken revelries in imitation of the Roman god Bacchus. Similarly, saturnalia honors Saturn, the Roman god of agriculture. Interestingly enough, though saturnalias are wild parties, a *saturnine* person is cold, gloomy and depressed.

scarify   To make superficial cuts or scratches. Certain African and Latin American tribes scarify their faces and bodies for decoration. The word can also be used in a figurative sense to mean making small insults, wounding with words. "The children scarified the new kid in the class by teasing him mercilessly about the way he dressed." Pronounced SCAR-*IF-EYE*.

scatology   The study of or excessive interest in excrement or obscenity, such as the works of William S. Burroughs or Laurence Sterne.

schwa — The upside-down *e* you always see in a dictionary. It denotes the sound similar to *eh*, as in *a*bout, *e*dible, circ*u*s. . . . Pronounced SHWAH.

scintilla — A spark or minute particle. It's usually accompanied by a modifier, as in, "not even a scintilla" or "not one scintilla." Pronounced SIN-*TILL*-AH.

scion — A child, in particular an heir. It's pronounced SIGH-ON.

scotch — Not just a whiskey. It means to wound without killing; to render harmless, such as shooting someone in the leg to prevent her escape.

scunner — Lots of people feel the victims of scunners. It means a dislike taken for no reason. If a teacher takes a scunner to you, you're in trouble.

scurrilous — Incredibly abusive, obscenely nasty. Villains are guilty of scurrilous deeds. This is a good word to use when you need to yell at someone who's made you furious, as in: "I'm sick and tired of your scurrilous treatment of me and everyone else around you." Say SCUR-*RIL*-USS.

sedulous — Someone who is sedulous is diligent and persevering and never gives up the ship, such as the Terminator, or, on the brighter side, the pioneers who settled the West. It's pronounced SEJ-*EH-LESS*.

semantics — The aspect of linguistics that is concerned with the meaning and usage of words. Being precise in what you say and how you say it is the greatest benefit of semantics. When someone's response to your argument is that you're just playing with semantics, they've decided to stop fighting about the facts, and to start accusing you of using double talk (which you would never do, of course).

seminal — Despite the *i*, the word derives from "semen," and means the source of a style, an idea or a philosophy. The Federalist Papers are a seminal work of American political thought; Einstein's work is seminal to modern physics. It's pronounced SEMM-*IN-AL*.

semiotics — The study of signs and symbols. Like linguistics, an oft-misunderstood yet fascinating field of study.

senescent — Aging, or becoming old. Generally used to describe people rather than things. Houses become decrepit;

people become senescent. Pronounced SEH-NESS-SENT.

sentientious

The word has two almost contradictory meanings: full of terse, pithy truths, or self-righteously moralizing and pedantic. Be careful how you use it. Pronounced SEN-TEN-SHUSS.

sequacious

Following smoothly or logically; happening in a sequence. A sequacious argument would be hard to argue with; a sequacious movie would be easy to follow.

serendipity

Serendipity is something wonderful that happens suddenly and unexpectedly, such as bumping into a dear friend 1,000 miles from home just after you've lost your traveler's checks.

serry

To crowd together closely. Sardines are packed, but people in an elevator are serried.

sesquipedalian

This is one of our favorites. It means a very long word (literally "a foot and a half"), or given to using very long words. A sesquipedalian loves using words like SESS-KWIH-PEH-DALE-YAN.

sexagenarian Aged between sixty and seventy years old. (See also *octogenarian*.)

shaman Literally, a shaman is a priest or witch doctor who uses supernatural powers in various tribal religions in Africa and Asia. The word is now used figuratively for any contemporary guru-type who exercises a kind of religious control over a set of followers. Jim Jones was a kind of shaman; some parents worry that certain heavy-metal rock stars are considered to be shamans by their young fans. Say *SHAH-MEN*.

shibboleth A doctrine or belief once held to be of great importance by a particular group or sect but now seen as rather old-fashioned and useless. Stoning witches and refraining from shopping on Sundays are both examples of shibboleths.

sibilant Any speech sound that resembles a hiss; in particular, words that begin with *s*, *z* or *sh*. Of course, it's all in the way you pronounce them. "Yes" is not necessarily sibilant, but could be: "'Yessssssssss, my pretty,' said the wicked witch." If you like, you can pronounce it *SSSSSSSSIB-EH-LANT*.

sic | Intentionally written. When used in printed materials, it means, "The person who wrote this article/letter/speech is an idiot; look at the mistake he made. But we the editors are smart, so don't blame us." Place it in parentheses after a misteak (sic). Sounds like *sick*.

sidereal | Relating to or determined by the stars. Astrologers profit from selling phony sidereal advice. Pronounced SYE-*DEER*-EE-AL.

simian | Resembling a monkey or ape in physical characteristics.

simpatico | In sympathy in ideas, manners or personalities. A successful computer-dating service puts simpatico people in contact. Say SIMM-*PAT*-EE-COH.

simulacrum | Deceptive likeness to or seeming similarity. Wax museums specialize in them. Pronounced SIM-YOOL-*AY*-CRUM.

sinecure | An office or post that provides honor or prestige and possibly even profit but which requires almost no work. Certain ambassadors' posts are considered sinecures, for example, because the job involves a lot of formal parties and official gatherings but very little political responsibility. It's pronounced *SIN-A-CURE*.

sine qua non   A Latin phrase for an indispensable requirement or essential need. Being a good host is the sine qua non for being the ambassador of good will for a country. It's pronounced *SEE-NAY KWA NON*.

sinistrodextral   Moving from left to right. An obvious example: written English is a sinistrodextral language; written Hebrew is not.

sipid   The opposite of *insipid* (tasteless) is a word in its own right. It means having a pleasing taste, flavor or character, such as a good full-bodied wine or a strong cheese.

sirenic   Having the qualities of a siren (the human kind)— women who are irresistibly alluring and almost dangerously tempting. Michelle Pfeiffer frequently plays sirenic roles. Pronounced *SY-REN-ICK*.

sitomanic   An abnormal or even neurotic craving for food. The next time you sit down with a spoon and a half gallon of ice cream, just grin and say you're having an attack of sitomania.

skulduggery   If you do something sneaky and underhanded, you are engaging in skulduggery. Though it's clearly dishonorable conduct, it's not as bad as an outright felony—you don't necessarily get thrown in jail for it. Filling your mom's purse with raspberry Jell-O is skulduggery. (Also spelled *skullduggery*.)

sloven   This is the noun for "slovenly." People who dress in a slovenly way are carelessly sloppy; sloven, therefore, is another word for slob. You can also use it as a name for someone who does a job poorly or haphazardly. The guy who came in to wash your windows and left great big streaks on the glass is a sloven. Pronounced *SLAH-VENN*.

slubber   To do hastily and carelessly. A *sloven* (see above) slubbers his work.

smarmy   Ingratiating; falsely flattering or fawning in order to get in someone's good graces. People without noticeable talent who need business are often smarmy, falling all over their clients. (See also *obsequious*.)

sniffish
Picture a haughty person with her nose in the air, sniffing disdainfully and staring contemptuously and you've got it—a sniffish snob.

snood
The Yuppie hairband made famous by Hillary Clinton is called a snood. Also a netlike cap worn by women. A snood was originally a badge of virginity. Now it just keeps your hair out of your eyes. Rhymes with *food*.

sobriquet
Moniker, another word for nickname. Chicago's sobriquet is "The Windy City." Pronounced SOH-BRICK-AY.

sociopath
A favorite insult to hurl at selfish, nasty, ungenerous and unthoughtful people, the word is a clinical term meaning someone who is hostile to society. Serial killers are often sociopaths.

sodality
Like *solidarity*, the word means companionship or union in attitude or belief. Two people who share common interests have a sodality between them.

soigné — Elegant in the sense of "well-groomed" or "carefully put together." A woman in a simple black dress with her hair arranged in a French twist (in the style of Audrey Hepburn or Catherine Deneuve) is soigné. It's pronounced SWAN-YAY.

soirée — From the French: a social gathering that takes place in the evening for a particular purpose, such as listening to live music, holding a discussion group or reading poetry. It has come to be used to mean any party held at night. Pronounced SWAR-AY.

solecism — Any mistake or inconsistency, including a grammatical error. A person who says "who" when he should say "whom," or "me" when he should say "I," speaks in solecisms. It's pronounced SOLL-EH-SIZ-EM. To pronounce it any other way would be a solecism.

solipsism — This philosophical theory asserts that the self is the only thing that exists or can be proved to exist, but its meaning has now been stretched to convey narcissism. Any person who sees him- or herself as the center of the universe may be called solipsistic.

somatist

A psychiatrist who believes that all mental illnesses are physical in origin. Almost the opposite of someone who believes that all illnesses are *psychosomatic*, or psychological in origin.

sonorous

Capable of producing deep, rich sound, like the bells of Notre Dame. Pronounced SAHN-OR-USS.

sophism

A deceptive or false argument or belief. When someone comes up with a series of facts that don't prove the point she's trying to make, you can accuse her of making a sophism. Say SOFF-IZM.

soporific

Something that produces sleep is a soporific. It can be used as a noun or an adjective. A sleeping pill is a soporific. A geography lecture may be soporific. (See also *saporific*, which has an entirely different meaning.)

sotto voce

These Latin words mean "in a whisper"—in a very low voice so as not to be overheard. Often seen in screenplays and stage directions. Use it as an adjective. " 'Blanche is a cow,' Hortense said *sotto voce* to her friend Hermione." Pronounced SOH-TOE VOE-CHAY.

sough

To make a sighing or rustling sound. Trees sough in a gentle wind. On a breezy day, the reeds along the edge of a pond sough. Pronounced SOW, not SUFF.

soupçon

The French word for a hint, a dash, a trace. It can be used in a recipe, such as a soupçon of brandy in the chowder, but it's commonly used figuratively as well. "The comedy was a delightful mix of terrific acting, slapstick humor and a soupçon of social parody." It's pronounced SOOP-SON, like when Mom or Pop calls the kid in for dinner.

spado

Another word for a castrated man or animal (see also *eunuch*). Literally. Rhymes with *Play-Dough*.

sparge

A sparge is a sprinkling or a spattering, like a sparge of wild lilies along the side of a highway. It can also be used as a verb, but it sounds more awkward than "scatter" or "sprinkle."

specious

Something that seems correct on the surface but turns out to be false or wrong. A specious argument sounds great but doesn't prove its point. It's pronounced SPEE-SHUSS.

spelunk	To explore caves. We wonder if spelunkers get their equipment in the same store as keglers do (see *kegler*). Note that if you need to know the difference between a stalactite (see *stalactite*) and a stalagmite, you should ask a spelunker. Say SPEH-*LUNK*.
spiniferous	Sounds like something that's either marvelous or delicious, but it's not. Blowfish and porcupines are spiniferous. The word means "covered with spines." Pronounced SPIN-*IFF*-ER-USS.
spoonerism	A spoonerism is the exchange of the first letter of two or more syllables or words with comic or clever results. This word comes from an English clergyman named W. A. Spooner who often made such slips of the tongue: "flutterby" for "butterfly," for example.
spoor	One of those words you hear often but are never quite sure what it means—a track or trail of bones, dung, or fur made by a person or an animal being hunted.
spurious	Not genuine; counterfeit. You could be talking about money or sympathy. If it's fake, it's spurious.

squib   A short, witty composition or saying, often an item
               in a newspaper. It also describes a short football kick.

stalactite   Not, of course, to be confused with *stalagmite*. Let's
               sort them out once and for all: a stala*ctite* is the
               icicle-like formation that hangs from the roof or wall
               of a cave. A stala*gmite* is a deposit on the floor of the
               cave that looks like an inverted stalactite. Remember
               that stalactites must be *tight* to stay on the roof of the
               cave and you'll be all set. Both are made from crystal-
               line calcium carbonate buildup.

stalwart   Stout; steady; dependably courageous. Friends who
               can be counted on for their bravery and loyalty
               are stalwart.

stentorian   People often use this word to mean authoritarian, but
               that's not exactly what it means. Someone who
               speaks with a stentorian voice speaks loudly and
               harshly. It often has the effect of being authoritarian,
               however.

stodge   To eat greedily; to gorge or stuff. People on diets
               often sneak down to the kitchen in the middle of the

night to stodge themselves with leftovers from the fridge.

stolid

Unemotional, or at least slow to express feelings. Certain men who were raised in the pre-consciousness-raising days are stolid. Old army officers who insist that their family members call them General, for instance, are also stolid. Pronounced *STAHL-ID*.

subaltern

Subordinate or of lower rank. It's used as an adjective. "The president and her subaltern staff toured the factory to see how the assembly-line workers were doing."

subjacent

Adjacent means side by side; so subjacent means lying directly under. "The basement of the house was subjacent to the living room." Say *SUB-JAY-SENT*.

subrogate

To substitute, as in subrogating fat-free foods for ice cream and butter when you're on a diet. When your history teacher was sick and you got a replacement for the day, she was not called a subrogate teacher because that's just not the idiom! Don't confuse subrogate with *surrogate*, which means more or less the same thing, but can be used as a noun.

subsume
To consider an idea, principle, theory or category as part of a larger whole. "Existentialism is subsumed by philosophy in the liberal arts class offerings at the university."

subterfuge
An evasion or deceit used to conceal or avoid something. High-school students use many forms of subterfuge in order to get out of physical education classes: they pretend to be sick, arrange to meet with a teacher or intentionally break a toe. It's pronounced *SUB-TER-FYOOJ*.

sui generis
A Latin phrase for "unique" or "one of a kind." You may claim an incredibly ugly antique vase that a pretentious relative gave you is a sui generis work of art. Opposite of generic. The correct pronunciation is *SOO-EYE JEN-ER-IS*.

sultry
Very hot and humid, like the air on a mid-August night in Miami, or sensual and voluptuous, like Rita Hayworth or Kathleen Turner.

summa cum laude
Latin for "with highest praise," the highest honor granted to exceptional graduates. (See also *magna cum laude*.) Pronounced *SOO-MA KUM LOUD-A*.

supercilious	Haughty, contemptuous or superior. (See also *bumptious*.) From the Latin word for "eyebrows." Pronounced SOO-PER-SILL-EE-US.
supernal	Celestial; heavenly; above ordinary human existence. Gods exhibit supernal powers; people with oversized egos think they do, too. Say SOO-PER-NULL.
surfeit	It's pronounced SIR-FIT, and it means an excess. The wealthy have a surfeit of assets.
susurrus	This word often crops up in highly descriptive prose. It means a gentle whispering or rustling, such as the sound of tall grass blowing in the wind or dry leaves dancing along pavement on an autumn day. It's pronounced a bit like the sound it describes: SOO-SIR-OOS. (See also *sough*.)
sybarite	A person who lives luxuriously and self-indulgently. Very posh resorts love to advertise as "a haven for sybarites." Say SIB-ER-ITE.
sylph	A slender, graceful woman. Audrey Hepburn is the prototype. Say it SIHLF.

synecdoche

A figure of speech in which a part is substituted for the whole, such as "Get your butt in here." (Obviously the speaker wants more than just your posterior.) Or the whole may be used to describe a part, as in "Big Business is responsible for polluting this lake." It's pronounced SIH-*NEK-DUH*-KEE.

synergy

Cooperative activity. Getting more than the sum of the parts. Synergy occurs in an office, for example, when coworkers give each other energy and inspire each other to be more creative and productive than they would be alone. Say *SIN-ER-JEE*.

T

taciturn

Preferring to remain silent; unwilling to talk. Children are often taciturn when they are asked to explain their behavior; adults are taciturn whenever they prefer to keep their feelings private. Taciturn people generally don't join group therapy unless they're trying to get over their unwillingness to talk to people.

talaria

The winged sandals worn by Mercury. Granted, Mercury and FTD are probably the only people who need to use this word regularly, but think about all those times you were in a hurry and wished you had a pair of talaria. Rhymes with *malaria*.

talisman

A lucky charm. Typically a rabbit's foot or any other doo-dad you habitually bring along when you're playing a team sport or gambling.

tatterdemalion   A person dressed in ragged clothing; possibly a decent alternative to "homeless person," except that a person in ragged clothing may very well have a home. The kids in the old "Our Gang" TV series were tatterdemalions.

telegenic   Sounds like a fortuneteller or someone with supernatural powers, but it's not. Someone who is telegenic looks good on television or, to use the more contemporary phrase, is videogenic.

teleology   The belief that all things in nature are created for a particular purpose. Evolution is all about teleology— the duckbilled platypus has developed a duckbill because it is useful in an overall natural design. Misused, this reasoning can give rise to statements like, "If man were meant to fly, he'd have wings." Pronounced TEL-EE-*AHL*-OH-JEE.

temblor   Another word for earthquake. Most often used by reporters in California in reporting on *yet another* earthquake. Note that the word is not *tremblor*, which may seem more accurate, but doesn't exist!

temerity

Daring, but meaning reckless or bold, more than brave. Someone who saves a mugging victim has courage; a student who talks back to a teacher has temerity.

tendentious

Not to be confused with *tenacious*, which means persistent. *Tendentious* means having a particular tendency; leaning; lacking impartiality. Tendentious people make poor judges.

tenebrous

Gloomy and dark. Stormy skies are tenebrous. So are the expressions on the faces of depressed people. Pronounced *TEN-EB-RUSS*.

tergiversation

Ambivalence; a continual changing of one's mind. Someone who can't decide what to wear to a party—or whether to go at all—is suffering a bout of tergiversation. It's pronounced *TER-JIV-ER-ZAY-SHUN*.

termagant

A violent, overbearing or shrewish woman. Some thought Joan Crawford fit this category. It's pronounced *TERM-AG-ENT*.

terrapin

An edible freshwater turtle. The name comes from the Algonquin Indians. Useful if you're ever offered turtle soup: "It has terrapins in it," you'll say.

theomania

Here's a great one to throw at that narcissistic friend of yours the next time you get in an argument. A theomaniac is someone who believes he is God or has been chosen by God for some special purpose. Distinguish from messianic (see *messianic*), which can have less heavenly associations.

thersitical

Verbally abusive; using foul language. When you hurl curses at someone, you are being thersitical. Pronounced THER-SIT-EH-KULL.

thespian

Anything relating to acting or the theatre. A small town's thespian society is responsible for the local theatre.

throe

It's pronounced *throw* but when it's spelled this way, it means a sharp pang of emotion. Adolescents frequently find themselves in the throes of despair; new lovers are usually in the throes of passion.

tiffin
: In India, millions of women prepare lunches each morning and send them by messenger to their husbands at work. This light midday meal is called a tiffin, and can now be used as an elegant way of describing the yogurt and apple you eat every day.

tilak
: The colored mark worn on the forehead by Hindu men and women. It's pronounced *TIL-IK*.

timorous
: Meek, fearful; another word for timid. Yes, you can be timorous as a mouse.

tintinnabulation
: The sound of ringing bells. The word often used as an example of onomatopoeia (see *onomatopoeia*) because it sounds just like what it means. Immortalized in Edgar Allan Poe's poem, "The Bells."

tonsorial
: This has nothing to do with those things in your throat that swell up when you're sick. Someone skilled in the tonsorial arts is a great barber.

toper
: Someone who drinks alcohol in excessive quantities is a toper and probably frequently slips into a torpor (see *torporific*). Rhymes with *doper*.

toothsome
Dentists are rarely toothsome. Toothsome means delicious or luscious: fresh peaches, perhaps, or a ripe avocado.

toponym
A name which is derived from the name of a place, such as Indiana Jones or Broadway Joe Namath. It's pronounced *TOP-OH-NIM*.

torporific
A lot like a soporific (see *soporific*). It means producing a state of inertia, called a *torpor*.

tortuous
This word does not mean causing torture; that's *torturous*. A tortuous road is a winding, twisting or crooked road; a tortuous argument is so convoluted that it's hard to follow.

traduce
To slander, malign, or ruin someone's reputation. Say *TRAH-DOOSE*.

transmogrify
To change in form or appearance, usually much for the worse. Dr. Jekyll transmogrified into Mr. Hyde. A simple project can transmogrify into a convoluted disaster when your boss's boss decides to change the objectives.

triage
An arrangement derived from medical situations that separates things into three categories of urgency—kill it, save it, or leave it where it is for the time being. Battlefield casualties are triaged. You can also approach decisions in a busy office the same way. It's pronounced TREE-AJ.

trilemma
Like a dilemma but with one extra problem—a situation in which there are three mutually exclusive alternatives.

trompe l'oeil
A painting intended to create an illusion. For example, a very realistic mural on the outside of a windowless building that gives the impression that windows exist. From the French for "deceiving the eye," it's pronounced TROMP LOY.

truculent
This is a very harsh word, though few people use it correctly. It means cruel, brutal, savage. The behavior of the Nazis during the Holocaust was truculent. It's pronounced TRUCK-YOO-LENT.

turbid
Opaque in the sense of muddy or clouded. This word is often confused with *turgid*, which means bloated,

swollen and pompous. Turgid prose can also be turbid prose, but these words do not mean the same thing.

turnback
The curved end of a clothes hanger. To prevent guests from stealing hangers, most hotels have replaced the turnback with a straight piece that fits into a hoop attached to the closet rod.

turtlet
A baby turtle. Cute, eh?

tyro
Also spelled *tiro* (both are correct), it means a beginner or novice. (See also *neophyte*.) Pronounced TIE-ROW.

U

ubiety

The opposite of absence, it means presence or the state of being there. Had Gertrude Stein known the word, she might have said of Oakland, "There is no ubiety there" instead of "There is no 'there' there"— but then she wouldn't have sounded like Gertrude Stein. Say YOU-BY-ET-EE.

ubiquitous

Appearing everywhere at the same time; omnipresent. During the Gulf War, yellow ribbons were ubiquitous. On commuter trains at rush hour, suits and ties are ubiquitous. Pronounced YOU-BICK-QUIT-US.

ultramarine

Not an underwater superhero. Deep blue in color.

ululate

To howl like a dog, hoot like an owl or wail like a coyote—the kind of sound friends make at 2:00 in the morning when they leave a bar, link arms and look up at the moon. It's pronounced *YOOL-YA-LATE*.

umbrage   The sense of being slighted or of having one's feelings hurt. You can take umbrage or give it. If someone calls you a silly fool, you would take umbrage at the remark—or possibly give umbrage for the remark and call her an idiot.

unctuous   Oily or slimy. Not a literal description as much as a way of describing someone's character. A person who is overly flattering or too smooth is unctuous. Lounge lizards, for example, are unctuous. Pronounced *UNK-SHUSS*.

unexceptionable   A nice word that should not be confused with *unexceptional*. Unexceptional means ordinary or average. Unexception*able* means without exception or fault; beyond criticism.

unseemly   Inappropriate; not in keeping with good taste. Walking into a fancy French restaurant without shoes on is unseemly behavior.

untoward

Very close to *unseemly* (see above). Untoward behavior is improper, not so much a question of good taste as of being rude. Pronounced UN-*TORD*.

urbane

Sophisticated, suave, worldly; at home in most social situations. Someone who knows which wine to order with which course, can read a menu in most languages and can maintain charming dinner-table conversation is urbane. Pronounced UR-*BAYNE*.

usury

The practice of lending money at illegally high interest rates. Even if not illegal, exorbitant rates (like those used for credit cards) can be described as usurious. Pronounced YOO-*ZHER-EE*.

uvula

The little glob of flesh that hangs down at the back of the mouth. You often see one wobbling when cartoon characters yell, and children always mistake it for a tonsil. It's pronounced YOOV-*YUH-LUH*.

uxorious

Completely enamored with one's wife, in fact overly so. A man who is completely submissive to his spouse is uxorious. It's pronounced UK-*SOR-EE-US*.

V

vacuous
Empty-headed; without ideas or purpose. It's often used to describe someone who is attractive but dumb. Chippendale's male strippers are a paradigm (see *paradigm*) for vacuity. Pronounced VAK-*you-us*.

vagary
A whimsical, capricious or eccentric idea or action. Pronounced VAY-*ger-ee*.

valetudinarian
This is not the smart student who makes a speech at graduation (that's a *valedictorian*). A valetudinarian is an invalid or a convalescing person who is obsessed with his poor health. Distinguish from a *hypochondriac*, who has the same feelings, but is healthy.

vassal
A subordinate. Not exactly a slave—more like a subject. From the feudal relationship between kings and their subjects. You could use the term sarcastically to refer to the boss's assistants.

239

vaunt — It means "to boast of" or "to brag about," and is usually used to describe a reputation. It is hard to get a reservation in a much-vaunted restaurant.

venal — Capable of being bribed; open to being corrupted. Pronounced *VEENL*.

venial — Contrary to popular misuse, a venial sin is one that *can* be pardoned, overlooked or forgiven. Distinguish from *venal* (see above), which is the Hall of Fame as far as sins go.

veracity — Truth. The veracity of something can be proven by hard evidence. Something that has veracity is *veracious*. This should not be confused with someone who is *voracious*, which means excessively eager, hungry for food or any other need.

verisimilitude — This is one of those words like juxtapose (see *juxtapose*) that people love to use in order to sound smart when criticizing art, literature or drama. It means the appearance of truth. So a film with verisimilitude does a good job of imitating life. Pronounced *VEHR-IH-SEH-MILL-EH-TOOD*.

vernal   Happening in the spring. For example, an equinox, or the budding of flowers, or the sighting of the first robin...

victress   Or *victrix*. A female victor, such as Joan of Arc, is a VICK-*TRESS*.

vigorish   This is a charge paid to a bookie for placing a bet; it can also refer to an interest fee paid to a money-lender.

virago   A fierce-tempered woman. "Hell hath no fury like a..." Well, virago. Pronounced VEH-*RAH*-GO.

vitiate   To impair or pollute or to make illegal or invalid. Toxic wastes can vitiate a body of water; cheating in a team sport vitiates the winning results. Say VISH-EE-ATE.

vituperative Violently abusive or fault-finding language, kind of like carping. When you bawl someone out, you use vituperative language. Pronounced VYE-*TOO*-PEH-RAY-TIV.

volitation
: The act of or capacity for flying. Birds have it; so does Superman. It's pronounced *VOLE-IH-TAY-SHUN*.

volition
: Free will. Doing something of your own volition means that you decided on your own to do it. You decided without outside aid or intervention.

voluble
: Someone who is voluble is talkative or loquacious. The word is generally used as a compliment to describe a friendly and verbal person. Use garrulous (see *garrulous*) for "overly talkative." A big mouth is garrulous; a talkative companion is voluble.

vulgate
: A popular word with literature buffs, it means the generally recognized or most used version of a work. The vulgate version of Shakespeare is the one professors assign most often.

vulpine
: Fox-like. Someone who is crafty or sneaky and seems to slip through your fingers is vulpine.

W

wallah wallah It means the same thing as muckity-muck or head honcho. A wallah wallah is the person in charge.

wamble Not what Elmer Fudd does in a motor home. To move unsteadily or stagger about. A drunk wambles down the street after a night at the bar. Say either *WOM-BULL* or *WHAM-BULL*.

wampus An unpleasant person, kind of like a lout. The lone heckler who keeps interrupting a great speech is a wampus.

wanton No, not a soup. Unprovoked, unjustified and generally egregiously out of control. Nasty people act with wanton disregard for the feelings of others; rioters may act with wanton destructiveness, breaking windows and looting shops. Say it *WAHN-TIN*.

warison   A note sounded to start an attack. This can be a
           literal trumpet call or a figurative battle cry. "When
           they decided to take separate vacations, I knew that
           was the warison for the divorce that followed."
           Pronounced *WAR-UH-SON*.

welt   A more powerful way to say "a bruise." Boxers often
           have welts after a difficult match.

Weltanshauung   A German word that means "world outlook" or
           "world view." It's a fancy way to say "perspective,"
           and if you use it correctly, it sounds intelligent but
           not pretentious. If you want to talk about small-town
           morality, you can talk about the town's *Weltan-
           shauung*. If you want to argue with someone, you can
           begin by saying "You have a different *Weltanshauung*"
           —you'll probably begin with an advantage. Make
           sure you pronounce it correctly: *VELT-AN-SHUNG*.

welter   A lot or a great many; confusion, turmoil. Imagine
           having a welter of homework to do or seeing a welter
           of dirty laundry scattered about your room. Also a
           verb that means to writhe or wallow.

Weltschmerz   The kind of word only the Germans could come up
               with. It literally means "world pain," but it's used to
               evoke a strong melancholy over the state of the
               world. Woody Allen exhibits *Weltschmerz* in most of
               his films; Ingmar Bergman does too, only without the
               humor. It's pronounced *VELT-SHMERTZ*.

whelk   An extremely civilized word for pimple, and a lot
               more euphonious (see *euphonious*) than "zit." Say
               WELK.

whiffle   There are several meanings for this word, but the best
               is "to vacillate or go back and forth about some-
               thing." Before going out to dinner, one may whiffle
               between wanting Chinese or Italian food.

white paper   An official report by the government about a specific
               issue. Environmentalists might refer to a white paper
               on the spotted owl.

winnow   It literally means to separate the grain from the chaff
               by getting rid of the chaff. There's even a piece of
               farm equipment called a *winnower*. You are more
               likely to use this word figuratively, however. You can

winnow out the weak athletes to make an all-star team, or winnow the unimportant books from your overcrowded shelves and give them away.

winsome
You lose some. (Just kidding.) This word means charming or attractive in a disarming way. It's pronounced WIN-SUM, and it's used to refer to both sexes.

witch ball
You probably know it as a disco ball, but this is the original word; it came before disco was even invented. A witch ball is one of those globes with many mirrored facets that hangs from the ceiling and sparkles as it rotates.

wittol
A variation on *cuckold*, a wittol is a man who knows about his wife's adultery and tolerates it. A cuckold is a man whose wife has been unfaithful, but he may not know about it.

wizened
Dried up and shriveled. An apple left in the sun too long is dried up; an old man's wrinkled face is wizened. Pronounced WIZ-END.

worm
: This isn't just the squiggly, slithering invertebrate. A worm is another word for the thread of a screw.

wraith
: A ghost. The word is supposed to mean a ghost that appears before a person to foretell his or her death, but it's now used more generally to refer to any apparition. The Ghostbusters, for instance, fought wraiths.

X

Xanadu
Originally a place of idyllic beauty in Samuel Coleridge's poem "Kubla Khan," it has come to refer to any place of idyllic beauty. For many people, Xanadu would be a beautiful cabin overlooking a mirror pond, surrounded by lush evergreens. Maybe that's why so many people have named their vacation homes Xanadu. Say ZAN-*AH-DOO*.

xebec
A three-masted sailing ship. A perfect word to use in *Scrabble* or *Ghost*. Or if you see a tall ship passing by, you can say, "Hey, there goes a ZEE-*BEK*."

xenophobia
Fear or hatred of foreigners, or of anything strange or foreign. It's pronounced ZEN-*A-FO-BEE-AH*.

xeric
Characterized by having or needing a very small amount of moisture. Deserts are xeric, as are many desert plants. It's said ZIR-*IK*.

X

Y

yahoo
The word comes from the name of a race of coarse and vulgar people invented by Jonathan Swift in *Gulliver's Travels*, but it has expanded over the past two centuries to mean any utterly gross person: a slob with no common courtesy is a yahoo. (See also *Lilliputian*.)

yatter
Like natter or patter, to make idle chatter. (What's the matter? You wish the definition were fatter?)

yegg
Not something you eat with yacon. A yegg is a petty burglar or common thug. What we generally refer to as a mugger can also be called a yegg.

yin and yang
You may know that these refer to the two universal forces in Chinese philosophy that are said to create the harmonious balance of nature and control the

destiny of all things, but do you know which is which? Yin is the dark, cold, still, and feminine aspect of things; Yang is the bright, warm, active and masculine aspect.

Z

zaftig

A Yiddish adjective that describes a woman who is pleasingly plump or well-rounded. Mae West is the queen of zaftig. It's pronounced ZOFF-TIG.

zarf

The holder for a handleless coffee cup. Though Styrofoam and cardboard have largely put zarfs out of business, you often see the plastic variety piled next to the office coffee machine.

zealous

Eager and diligently devoted; ardent. A zealous worker comes in at the crack of dawn and works till the wee hours of the night to get a job done as thoroughly and perfectly as possible. A *zealot*, on the other hand, is someone who is devoted to a fault—a fanatic. Say ZELL-US and ZELL-UT.

Zeitgeist
: Another great German word, in the spirit of *Weltanshauung* and *Weltschmerz*, that has broad philosophical implications. It means "spirit of the times," and refers to the general cultural, moral, and intellectual climate of a particular era. It's pronounced ZITE-GUYST.

zith
: The word literally refers to the point on the celestial sphere that is directly above the observer at any given location, and is therefore the highest point. It is the opposite of the nadir (see *nadir*), which is directly below. It is used to refer to any highest point, as in the zenith of someone's career or life.

zephyr
: A gentle breeze. It might blow through the trees and grasses, soughing and creating susurruses (see *sough* and *susurrus*).

zinfandel
: A pink or white wine that people like and wine critics don't. Made from a small black grape, usually in California. Pronounced ZIN-FEHN-DELL.

zoanthropy
: A mental illness in which the patient believes he is an animal. A woman says to a psychiatrist, "My

husband has believed he's a chicken for the last four years." "Why'd you wait so long to come to me?" he asks. "We needed the eggs." That's zoanthropy. Pronounced ZOE-*AN*-THREP-EE.

zoetrope

The forerunner of the motion picture, a zoetrope is a device consisting of a drum inside which is placed a series of images representing successive positions of a moving object. When the drum is rotated rapidly, the images, seen through slits on the walls of the drum, give an illusion of motion. This is the conceptual breakthrough that led to the development of motion pictures. It's also the name of Francis Ford Copolla's film company. (Now you can say you know *everything*.) Pronounced ZOH-*EH*-TROPE.

zoology

The science of animal study. There is no "zoo" in zoology—next time you need to say it, the correct pronunciation is ZOH-*AHL*-OH-JEE.

zugzwang

Chess enthusiasts probably know this word because it means a situation in a game of chess where all the moves open to one player will cause damage to his position. Like many chess moves, it's an excellent word to use metaphorically. It's pronounced *TSOOK-TSFANG*.

zwieback

Sweetened bread, cooked twice and sliced thin. Usually used by teething youngsters to give them something to do with their newfound teeth. Say *ZWEE-BACK*.

zygote

A term from cellular biology, generally used in conversation to refer to the cell that results from the meeting of the egg and the sperm. Father to son: "I've known you ever since you were a zygote." Pronounced *ZYE-GOAT*.

About the Authors

SETH GODIN is President of Seth Godin Productions, a book packaging firm with more than 40 titles to its credit. His work has ranged from books on stain removal and business to how-to volumes on Nintendo games. Seth enjoys *Pictionary* and *Scrabble*, but his ear for trivia and weird words make him no fun to play with. He lives in Westchester, New York, with his wife, Helene, and their very smart dog, Lucy.

MARGERY MANDELL is an Editor at Seth Godin Productions. She also teaches journalism at New York University and the Sarah Lawrence College Writing Institute. In her spare time, she travels the world as a freelance journalist, reporting for several international publications. Margery lives in Westchester, New York, with her husband, Mark, and their children, Jacob, Alix, and Katie.